Grounded
by
GRANITE
a memoir

A coming of age tale of family
connection and personal resilience
framed by summers on a remote
island in the Canadian Shield

Patti Shales Lefkos

LOON
ISLAND
PRESS

LOON ISLAND PRESS
Box 3093
Vernon, BC, Canada.
V1B 3M1.

Library and Archives Canada Cataloguing in Publication
Title: Grounded by Granite: *A coming of age tale of family connection
and personal resilience framed by summers on a remote island in the
Canadian Shield/* Patti Shales Lefkos
Names: Shales Lefkos, Patti, author
Identifiers: Canadiana
Grounded by Granite - Print - ISBN 978-1-9992298-2-5

Cover design by Mishell Raedeke
Cover photo by William E. Shales
Interior design by Mishell Raedeke
Interior photos by William E. Shales, Patti Shales Lefkos, Barry Hodgins
Edited by Sylvia Taylor
Printed and bound in Canada

In memory of
Elizabeth Leatherland
1831 - 1863

For

Walter Douglas Shales and Anne
Kathleen Wright Gordon Shales
Gordon Douglas Shales
Donna Anne Gordon Shales

And, of course, Roger.

There is a transcendent power in a strong
intergenerational family. An effectively
interdependent family of children, parents,
grandparents, aunts, uncles, and cousins
can be a powerful force in helping people
have a sense of who they are and where they
came from and what they stand for.

—*Stephen R. Covey, The 7 Habits of Highly Effective People*

**In recognition of the First Nations
on whose territory the Shales family settled.**

"The Frontenac Arch biosphere region overlaps the traditional territories
of the Anishinaabe (Algonquin) and Haudeno saunee (Iroquois)
lands and covers an area from Brockville and Gananoque, extending
north of Kingston including Harrowsmith, Vernon and Westport."
frontenacbiosphere.ca

Also by Patti Shales Lefkos
Nepal One Day at a Time:
One Woman's Quest to Build a School in the Remote Himalaya

CONTENTS

CONTENTS

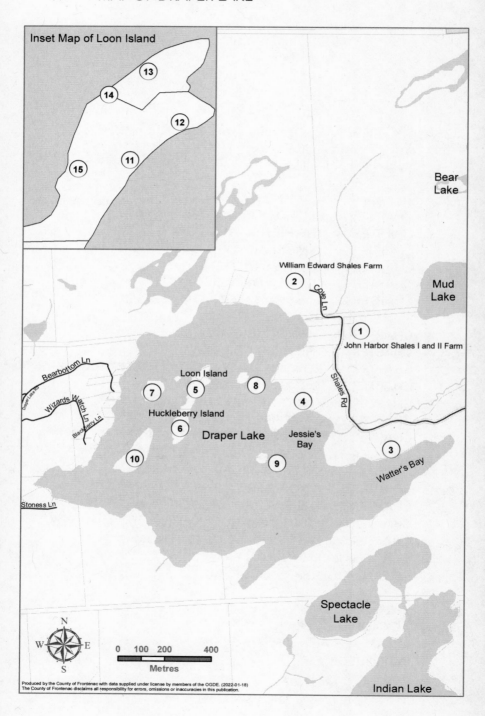

Inset Map of Loon Island

Bear
Lake

Mud
Lake

William Edward Shales Farm

John Harbor Shales I and II Farm

Loon Island

Huckleberry Island

Draper Lake

Jessie's
Bay

Watter's Bay

Spectacle
Lake

Stoness Ln

Bearbottom Ln

Wizards Watch Ln

Blackberry Ln

Cove Ln

Shales Rd

Indian Lake

Metres

0   100   200   400

Produced by the County of Frontenac with data supplied under license by members of the OGDE. (2022-01-18)
The County of Frontenac disclaims all responsibility for errors, omissions or inaccuracies in this publication.

1. John Harbor Shales I and II farm (first settlers)

2. William Edward Shales, 3rd generation farm (later
    Elwood and Alice Shales 4th generation)

3. Walter and Hazel Shales summer cottage
    (now owned by Ian Shales)

4. Jessie and Charlie Shales farm (now
    owned by the Traversy family)

5. Loon Island (Doug and Anne Shales, now
    owned by Patti and Doug Shales)

6. Huckleberry Island (Dave and Gladys Shales,
    now owned by David Shales Jr.)

7. Stonehouse Island (Jack and Laura Shales,
    now owned by the Robinson family)

8. Sunset Island and cottage (William Elmo and Spray Shales,
    Patti's grandparents, now owned by Doug and Margo Shales)

9. Turkey Island (Leighfield family, now owned by
    Drue Shales, Gary Pollenz and Scott Smith)

10. Birch Island (Crown Land)

11. Front Rock and lawn (Granite home base)

12. First Rock (fish cleaning and turtle hunting)

13. Second Rock (Donna and Bruce McFarlane's cottage,
    later Donna Shales and Arthur Pigeon)

14. Turtle Rock

15. Third Rock (Patti Shales Lefkos and Barry Hodgins cottage)

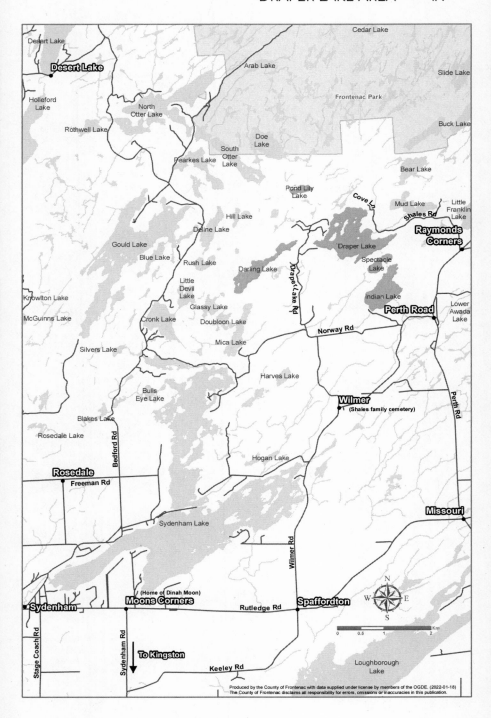

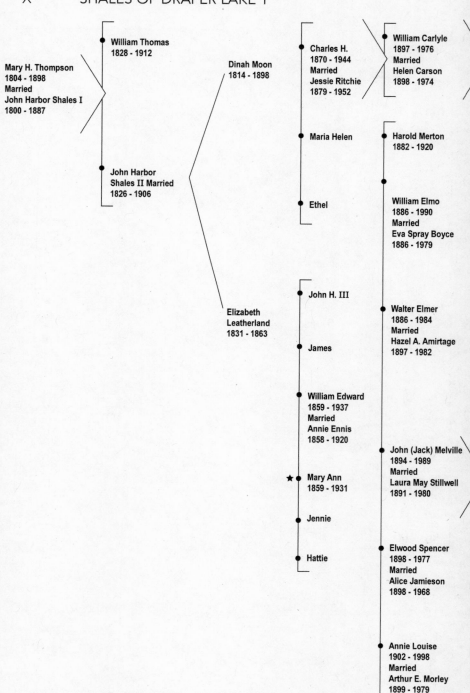

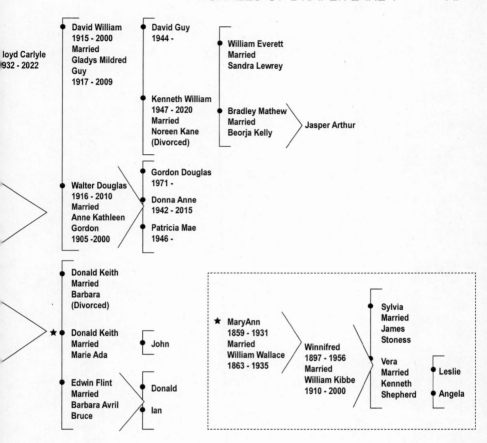

loyd Carlyle
932 - 2022

David William
1915 - 2000
Married
Gladys Mildred
Guy
1917 - 2009

David Guy
1944 -

William Everett
Married
Sandra Lewrey

Kenneth William
1947 - 2020
Married
Noreen Kane
(Divorced)

Bradley Mathew
Married
Beorja Kelly

Jasper Arthur

Walter Douglas
1916 - 2010
Married
Anne Kathleen
Gordon
1905 -2000

Gordon Douglas
1971 -

Donna Anne
1942 - 2015

Patricia Mae
1946 -

Donald Keith
Married
Barbara
(Divorced)

★ **Donald Keith**
Married
Marie Ada

John

Edwin Flint
Married
Barbara Avril
Bruce

Donald

Ian

★ **MaryAnn**
1859 - 1931
Married
William Wallace
1863 - 1935

Winnifred
1897 - 1956
Married
William Kibbe
1910 - 2000

Sylvia
Married
James
Stoness

Vera
Married
Kenneth
Shepherd

Leslie

Angela

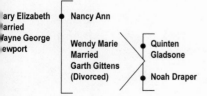

aula

ohn Stillwell
922 - 2004

ary Elizabeth
arried
Wayne George
ewport

Nancy Ann

Wendy Marie
Married
Garth Gittens
(Divorced)

Quinten
Gladsone

Noah Draper

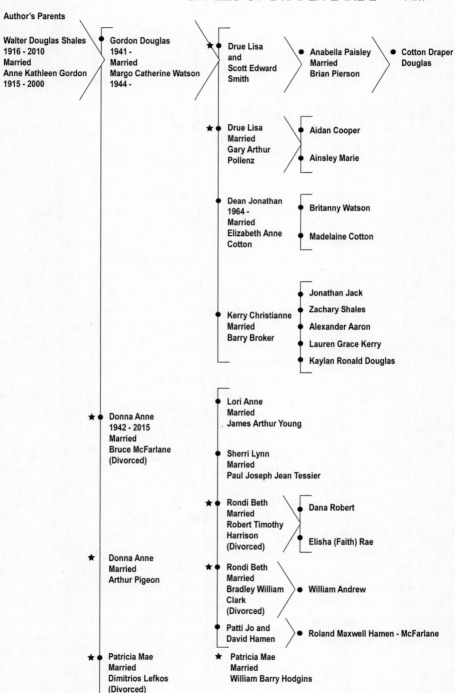

Author's Parents

Walter Douglas Shales
1916 - 2010
Married
Anne Kathleen Gordon
1915 - 2000

Gordon Douglas
1941 -
Married
Margo Catherine Watson
1944 -

★ Drue Lisa
and
Scott Edward
Smith

Anabella Paisley
Married
Brian Pierson

Cotton Draper
Douglas

★ Drue Lisa
Married
Gary Arthur
Pollenz

Aidan Cooper

Ainsley Marie

Dean Jonathan
1964 -
Married
Elizabeth Anne
Cotton

Britanny Watson

Madelaine Cotton

Kerry Christianne
Married
Barry Broker

Jonathan Jack
Zachary Shales
Alexander Aaron
Lauren Grace Kerry
Kaylan Ronald Douglas

★ Donna Anne
1942 - 2015
Married
Bruce McFarlane
(Divorced)

Lori Anne
Married
James Arthur Young

Sherri Lynn
Married
Paul Joseph Jean Tessier

★ Rondi Beth
Married
Robert Timothy
Harrison
(Divorced)

Dana Robert

Elisha (Faith) Rae

★ Donna Anne
Married
Arthur Pigeon

★ Rondi Beth
Married
Bradley William
Clark
(Divorced)

William Andrew

Patti Jo and
David Hamen

Roland Maxwell Hamen - McFarlane

★ Patricia Mae
Married
Dimitrios Lefkos
(Divorced)

★ Patricia Mae
Married
William Barry Hodgins

INTRODUCTION

Following a rewarding career in education I earned a diploma in Journalism at Langara University in 2007 at the age of 60. I thought my post-education life would consist of writing occasional freelance magazine and newspaper articles. But then my husband Barry and I ramped up our goal of international adventure travel. When we attended the Book Passage Travel Writers and Photographers Conference in San Francisco a whole new career opened for me. Still, I never imagined I would write a book, let alone two. But, here I am inviting you in to the pages of my second book, *Grounded by Granite*.

In 2008, after breaking in our hiking boots on the Coast to Coast hike in England's Lake District, we tested our tolerance to high altitude on Tibet's Mount Kailash circumambulation. In 2011 we spent three exhilarating months in Nepal trekking the Annapurna Circuit and the Annapurna Sanctuary. We discovered the dusty, windy trails of the forbidden kingdom of Upper Mustang and later followed the rocky route to Everest Base Camp.

Three years later, when various friends and family experienced frightening illnesses and Barry ruptured his Achilles tendon, I made the difficult decision to return to Nepal, this time for a solo volunteering and trekking adventure. During that trip, on a visit to remote Aprik village in Gorkha, the village elders requested my assistance to build a school. Back at home Barry and I formed the British Columbia non-profit Nepal One Day at a Time Society and I started writing articles about my solo travels. Then, in 2015 an earthquake registering 7.8 on the Richter scale devastated much of Nepal, killing more than 8,000 people. Every home in Aprik village, close to the epicenter of the earthquake, lay in heaps of rubble. Fundraising began in earnest. It was time to tell the story.

I launched the resulting book, *NEPAL ONE DAY AT A TIME, One Woman's Quest to Build a School in the Remote Himalaya,* on March 12, 2020, at the Caetani Cultural Centre in Vernon, BC, the day before the Covid-19 lockdown took effect. Without warning we were all hunkered down at home, connecting on Zoom. We thought it would last only a few weeks. When it didn't, I climbed the steep learning curve of how to market a book online. I muddled through with Facebook the best I could.

By June the writing was on the wall. Our annual flight to our summer cottage near Kingston, Ontario was out of the question. A sixth-generation Draper Lake resident, I had rarely missed a summer on our family's Loon Island. The blues set in. Then I felt guilty for being sad. After all, I live in the safe, peaceful woods at SilverStar Mountain, a resort in British Columbia's Okanagan Valley. Hardly a bad place to be stuck. I hiked through alpine flowers each day. We bought inflatable stand-up-paddleboards but the frantic motorboat traffic of the Okanagan Lakes unnerved me. I longed to visit family, swim in the quiet, pristine waters of Draper Lake and warm my bare feet on the sun-kissed granite of our island. But, at that point, stepping into an airplane seemed too risky.

My outlook changed when September 2020 rolled around. I discovered Chandler Bolt's Self-Publishing School. Familiar with Zoom by this time, I signed up for Author Advantage Live, his annual conference about writing, self-publishing and marketing books. Chandler's team and the discovery of Hal Elrod's book, *Miracle Morning* inspired me. Re-energized I began every morning with Hal's routine-SAVERS: silence, affirmations, visualization, exercise, reading and scribing (journal writing). With Chandler's template as a base, I pitched and signed on for numerous podcast appearances and landed Zoom book club presentations to promote my book *NEPAL ONE DAY AT A TIME*.

Still, my heart longed for our island retreat. I dreamt of childhood summers, the idyllic family times when it felt like our extended family owned the entire lake and modern intrusions like electricity would never reach the island. I spent hours talking and laughing on the phone with my brother Doug, in Oakville Ontario, rehashing memories. I studied black and white photos: our family in the canoe, mom in shorts and a halter top at the cottage door, a gaggle of extended family and guests gathered on the granite swimming rock. I began to realize the gift of the grounding and resilience created by those early experiences.

The pandemic continued. During the winter we went cross-country skiing and snowshoeing through silent woods. We kept to ourselves. For me it was a time of self-isolation, sitting at my office desk, writing, lost in stories of the cottage. By spring I felt desperate for my island heart-home. We got our vaccinations and set out for the 4,200 kilometre drive from Vernon, BC to Kingston, Ontario, halfway across Canada.

Filled with gratitude, I felt new appreciation when we pulled into the parking field on the shore of Draper Lake, loaded the canoe with luggage and groceries and paddled the less than a kilometre distance to our island home. Every outdoor deck gathering with family held new significance. Every tall maple or cedar seemed more precious than before. Swimming excursions from the granite Front Rock in front of our original family cottage with my nieces seemed more ceremonial than ever. I spent hours with distant cousins, Mary, Vera and Ian, sharing thoughts of our connection to the land. I spent days dreaming of the past, enjoying the present and visiting traditional family haunts, then from late June to mid-October immersed myself in writing about it all.

The result is a book filled with stories of a cottage life that I hope will bring your own treasured memories into focus or inspire possibilities of future cottage dreams. Thanks to my older brother Doug for igniting the spark for me to recall incidents long buried in my psyche. He provided details from his perspective as an older brother, often filling in blanks for me. His vivid descriptions of days spent in the fields and barns of the Shales family farm paint a picture of a bygone era.

We all experience and remember things differently. The stories in *Grounded by Granite* are written from my point of view. The episodes I have chosen to highlight are the ones that stand out in my memory as the youngest of three siblings. These are the events that affected me most and shaped who I am today. Some of the names of people have been changed.

In 2023, Barry and I plan to return to Nepal to build two homes lost in the earthquake and continue our work with the school community in Aprik Village. We also plan to spend a month trekking in Upper Dolpo, a remote kingdom near the border of Tibet.

In the meantime, I leave you with the stories that grounded me, helped to make me a adventurer and an environmentalist. My heart is full of appreciation for my ancestors, my extended family and the magical place that shaped me as a woman physically strong and mentally determined enough to continue to trek with her mountaineering husband or travel the world solo.

PROLOGUE
July 17, 2010

"**S**wimmers, take your mark," I holler over my shoulder. The laughter and chatter behind me continue as I turn back toward the lake.

Hot, humid and hazy. Canadians across the country are flocking to national parks to celebrate the 125th anniversary of Parks Canada. For us it's a typical summer afternoon on Loon Island in Draper Lake. There are three generations, aged seven to seventy, descendants of 1868's lakeshore farmer John Harbor Shales. Some have travelled thousands of miles to gather at this prized portion of the Canadian Shield, known to family as the Front Rock.

I step off the cool grass. The soles of my feet absorb the warmth of the rock. Coarse granite takes me back to the stubbed toes and skinned knees of childhood. No more reckless scampers headlong down the rock, splashing through the shallows for a dive off the edge. Now, I lower myself, one leg at a time, to a sitting position on the worn boards of the floating dock. Rough-sawn boards, bleached and slivered, have weathered almost as many summers as I have. The warm lake water tickles my knees as I step into the shallow.

More than sixty years ago my parents chose this location for our cottage because the island's twenty-metre-long ledge of rock, a combination of quartz, feldspar and mica beckoned as the perfect spot to learn to swim. Its grey, multi-textured surface rolls gently into the water, sloping gradually like a man-made pool from ankle deep to chest high before dropping off sharply into what the youngest swimmers refer to in hushed tones as "the black water." Regular treatment with a stiff-bristled barn brush creates a slip-free, barefoot-friendly surface and keeps the water clear for underwater sunfish surveillance.

Already dressed for swimming, the troupe of sons, daughters, nieces, nephews, cousins and grandchildren stands frozen in time on the lawn, a summer still life, a textbook tableau of the ideal Ontario cottage afternoon. Each hesitates a moment, then one at a time they fling croquet mallets aside, abandon badminton racquets on the grass, take one last hot sip of tea and return their Blue Willow teacups to the patio table.

"Can I go today?" All eyes turn to seven-year-old Alex. He has decided to try his first attempt of the 400-metre crossing from Loon Island to his grandfather's island.

" Okay. But, you know the rule. If you have to touch the boat during the swim, you have to get in," his mom Ker says.

"I know," Alex says. "I'll be fine." He looks down, his smile self-assured as he fastens his goggles.

"I'll row." My perennial-lifeguard brother Doug sets down his mug of tea and gets up from his lawn chair. He stuffs three chocolate chip cookies into the pocket of his shorts, shoots me a boyish grin and heads for the rowboat.

"Last call. Swimmers take your mark," I shout one last time.

One by one the water babies line up beside me in the shallows along the drop off. Each adult declares the name of the budding athlete they will monitor.

"I'm on Alex," Ker says.

"I've got Aidan," I say. My grand-nephew Aidan, who has just gained teen status, turns toward me.

"Yeah, right." His brief attempt to curl his lip in an age-appropriate derisive sneer switches to a mischievous smirk. He's just completed lifeguard training. He's sure this is the year he will finally beat me across.

"I'm with Donna," my husband Barry says. Early onset dementia has reduced my only sister's energetic front crawl to a tentative yet smooth breaststroke. Still, Donna, four years older than I am, never misses a family swim.

Neither do I. Hardly ever. Side-by-side, Doug, Donna and I have been pushing off for the inter-island swim almost every summer of our lives. I am more myself at the lake than anywhere else on earth. After completing university and starting my teaching career in Toronto, I moved West in 1975. I married a fellow British Columbia teacher, an outdoor enthusiast and paddler with superb cottage building skills. Turned out to be a good decision, in many ways. Every summer when the island beckons my heart home, my outdoor guy is game for the trip East.

Doug launches our grandpa's ancient red wooden boat, rows out into the lake and hovers off the rock ledge. Toes push us off into the deep. Chatting and laughing the unruly mob of fifteen swimmers sets out toward the other island. After a few strokes, my triathlon training kicks in. I fall naturally into the rhythm of breathing every third stroke. I glance up to sight on the tall pine tree on the corner of Doug's island every thirty rotations. Each time I turn to the right, my eyes connect with Aidan's. I pick up the pace. So does he. His arms, now longer than mine, stretch out, slipping expertly into the surface. With one big breath, one last push, I surge ahead.

My toes search down through the shoreline weeds for my usual underwater rock to stand on. Still breathing heavily, I turn to Aidan.

"What happened?"

"I let you go ahead. There might be snakes and snapping turtles."

"You're such a pathetic pool swimmer!" I splash some water in his face. He dodges and returns my tease with a look that takes me back in time, his grin reminiscent of my only brother, his grandfather.

Others catch up, find a rock perch in the weedy shallows or

tread water slightly offshore. All group members accounted for, Ker turns to Alex.

"What do you think? Want to swim back?"

Alex stares into the water with more than a smidgen of seven-year-old scorn. "Mom. It's what you do."

"Go ahead," I say to Ker. "I've got Alex."

Tanned arms, muscled from water polo and lifting children, strike out for the return trip. She and Aidan lead the way back to our sun-warmed, confidence-building base camp. Alex and I touch the rock last to the cheers of waiting relatives.

Every season starts with dog-paddle lessons in the shallows, progresses to the first frightening foray into the deep, then rapidly morphs into front crawl finesse and the privilege of joining the multi-generational distance swims. An ever-increasing number of lifeguards, swim and sailing instructors, camp counselors, canoe guides and bass fishermen have launched summer jobs and careers from this coarse-grained igneous foundation – the bedrock that every summer calls them home.

My siblings and I are the only ones left of our generation. Now Doug and I alone hold the memory of several childhood winters of fear and heartache, the terrifying realization of how close we came to losing this crucial hunk of adhesive that cements our widely-dispersed clan, Loon Island.

CHAPTER 1
BEACH GIRL GOES WILD

August 1948

Dad and my brother Doug steered the canoe toward an uninhibited island, a pristine portion of the Canadian Shield. Dad's parents had presented Mom and Dad with the one-and-a-half-hectare parcel of paradise on their wedding day.

The hull of Miss Niagara glided smoothly, her shiny bow slicing a perfect V through the water. My paternal grandfather, William Shales, had discovered the slick cedar strip canoe advertised second hand in the Kingston Whig Standard newspaper in 1928. He pledged $15. Dad and his brother Dave each contributed $15 from their paper route earnings. Two teen-aged brothers, one canoe, countless summer adventures.

But that summer Miss Niagara was all ours. Dad manned the stern. My big brother Doug, seven, paddled bow. He shared the seat with Mom who faced back toward Dad. My big sister Donna, aged six, and I shared space in the bilge.

Moments later Dad nosed the canoe through a jumble of white water lilies, waving in graceful welcome. He wedged the bow between bulrushes, then skillfully rotated the stern. The canoe came to rest parallel to the shore. He stood and stepped out onto dry land, grinning ear to ear.

"Here we are, finally. Give me your hand, Anne."

Mom stood. The canoe shuddered. Donna and I clutched the gunwales for stability. We weren't used to riding in a canoe. Mom hesitated, regained her balance and peeked tentatively through the dense wall of scrub cedars.

She clutched Dad's hand. "Are there bears?"

"Maybe a few beaver and the occasional possum. That's about it."

Dad sounded like the canoe guide he once was, casually trying to calm young female campers. His brown eyes shone with hope and anticipation as Mom took that first brave step.

While Dad was at home in the woods, bushwhacking didn't rate high on Mom's summer vacation to-do list.

"I was a beach girl," she said, years later, whenever the story came up around the dinner table. "I came from the vast open expanse of Bruce Beach with a distant view of Ontario's Lake Huron whitecaps. I was more at home in tennis whites on clay courts than in a plaid shirt paddling a canoe."

Dad always followed with. "Your mom took five steps, fighting her way into the thick underbrush. She swatted a few mosquitoes, agreed that spot would be fine, then beat a hasty retreat back to the canoe."

It was mid-August, around the time of my second birthday. At least, that's what I've been told. I'm not sure what I remember of that auspicious day, if anything. What I think of as memories may well be familiar stories invented from gazing time and again at the one faded black and white image of the five of us in the canoe. Each time I came upon that photo the story changed, depending on the narrator. Whatever the truth, we never tired of the story, somehow sensing how meaningful it was to our family.

After that brief visit to the island Dad and Doug silently paddled us toward an adjacent one-acre mound of forested granite, clearly visible from the family farm currently run by Grandpa's younger brother Elwood and his wife Alice on the shore of Draper Lake. The small island housed a modest summer cottage built by Grandpa Shales and his wife, Spray,

Doug and Anne with Doug Jr, Donna and Patti in Miss Niagara. —Will Shales 1948

my grandmother. As we approached the dock, Grandpa called out.

"Stop paddling for a minute."

Grandpa, a science teacher and amateur photographer, raised his camera to his eye. Dad and Doug put down their paddles. We all turned to face Grandpa. No sunglasses, we squinted against the sun.

"We've just been over to our island to find a good spot for camping next summer." Dad's eyes radiated excitement. Mom's expression mirrored that of a timid fawn.

Grandpa snapped the photo.

I often wonder what someone seeing that photo for the first time might think. Five people enjoying a family outing, we are bareheaded in the late afternoon sun, not a life jacket in sight. Mom's straight blond hair shows the results of a recent altercation with Toni Home Permanent. It must have been Mom who braided Donna's wavy sun-bleached blond hair. Dad hardly ever did our hair, except for winter Sundays when Mom went to church early because she sang in the choir. He had the most trouble brushing my strawberry-blond hair, naturally curly like his.

What can we learn from the seating arrangement? Why are Dad and Doug paddling while Mom and Donna sit idle? A sign of the times? Maybe it's a statement of letting the oldest or the boy of the family lead the way. Or is it just Doug's turn to paddle? Will Donna take the bow seat next time? Why is Mom wearing a flowered sundress with a fluffy collar if an expedition to explore our island was the plan? Has she dressed me in a sun suit with ruffles because she hopes I'll grow up to be a girly girl who will share her penchant for frills?

Eight years earlier Mom and Dad had honeymooned on our grandparents' island. They arrived in Miss Niagara, jammed to the gunwales with camping supplies. Dad's two-week vacation provided Mom with a preview of island camping. One blackened pot for cooking oatmeal porridge, charred wieners roasted on green maple sticks over an open fire and nights on a thin, lumpy camp mattress sheltered by an already aging canvas army tent. Dad was in his element, reliving adventures from summer employment as a canoe guide at Taylor Statten's camps, Ahmek and Wapomeo, in Algonquin Park in south-central Ontario 260 kilometres west of Ottawa.

In stark contrast, Mom, a beach girl, summered at her family's cottage on Bruce Beach, a vibrant cottage community on the shore of Lake Huron, near Kincardine, Ontario. A United Church minister, her father, Reverend James Wesley Ross Gordon was assigned a new church in a different Ontario town every four years. Summers at Bruce Beach remained a constant throughout her childhood. A parade of stylish outfits defined her days. Mornings found her in tennis togs, white shirts and short skirts. A fierce competitor she reveled in placing ace serves and nasty shots against all comers on the red clay courts. In the afternoon she and her sister Alison wore modest early 1930s bathing suits to splash among the crashing waves. The sisters sported halter-tops and high-wasted wide-leg floral shorts for late day driving lessons on the hard beach sand with their older brother Doug. She and Alison often rushed dinner in time to slip into filmy summer dresses, then wiled away warm evenings on the sprung dance floor at the Kincardine Pavillion.

Mom and Dad fell in love at the University of Western Ontario. Mom, a petite tennis team member and nursing student; Dad,

William Edward Shales, John Melville Shales, Harold Merton Shales, William Elmo Shales (author's grandfather) Annie Ennis Shales, Walter Elmer Shales - circa 1896

a tall math and business double major starred as place kicker for the Western Mustangs football team.

Honeymooning in a leaky tent on a rocky island surrounded by an abrupt drop to the depths of a chilly lake challenged her at first. Well, maybe for quite a while. None of us were around then to hear those conversations. Just as well. Dad said he did most of the cooking. In the one photograph that remains of that time, two slim, tanned young lovers peer out from the opening of the tent between the pines. Maybe Dad looks more at home than Mom. It's hard to tell. One thing is for sure, their dreamy, self-satisfied expressions indicate true love.

The Canadian Shield, a vast area of exposed Pre-Cambrian igneous and metamorphic rock formed the core of the North American continent. The land, once scraped by glaciers retained only a thin layer of soil on granite rock. It made farming a tough proposition. Mixed, barely subsistence farming including dairy and beef cattle, chickens, pigs and vegetable gardening was the best my ancestors from England, the first farm settlers on the shore of Draper Lake, John Harbor Shales and his wife Mary Thompson, could hope for. They created a legacy of Shales resilience grounded by a tradition of fortitude and hard work.

My Grandpa Shales, a third generation Canadian of British Ancestry, was born in 1886 in a log house on the shore of Draper Lake. When he was ten his father, William Edward Shales built a large Victorian frame farmhouse to accommodate his growing family. Grandpa, William Elmo Shales and his three brothers, his identical twin Walter, brothers Harold and John and later his little sister Louise had a clear view of the islands from the kitchen of the house. Over his bowl of steaming oatmeal laced with maple syrup from the sugar bush, Grandpa pulled his chair up to the kitchen table beside the wood stove, gazed out over the lake and dreamed of someday building a cottage on one of the islands. When he neared retirement he and Grandma, Eva Spray

Boyce Shales, purchased the small rocky island in direct view of the farmhouse kitchen. A few years later, in the early 30s, they decided to stretch the budget far enough to purchase an island for each of their sons.

Clarence Stoness, a local farmer, owned the long expanse of shoreline abutting the 200 hectare Shales farm. One long island rested inside the boundaries of his farm concession. In the early 1900s, the lake level rose when local farmers dammed the outlet creek to accommodate a sawmill, the property appeared as two separate islands. By the time Grandpa purchased the land from Clarence Stoness the sawmill had been decommissioned. The dam was removed, the outlet creek allowed to flow freely and the level of the lake considerably reduced. One long island divided itself into two almost separate properties. Marshy lowland connected two sections of higher ground, each of about four acres. Grandpa sealed a quit claim deal, legally transferring ownership of the islands to Grandpa. Money changed hands. Both he and Clarence Stoness considered the transaction fair and sound.

On the day of our trip to Loon Island we'd been at the lake for a few weeks. Dad had arranged accommodation at his parents' cottage and in newly constructed cottages on the farmland waterfront conducive to Mom's comfort level. The romance of honeymoon camping faded when children arrived. The idea of camping with three kids on an island didn't appeal to her.

We spent the first week on the same island where Mom and Dad honeymooned in 1938. But, this time we bunked in with our Grandma and Grandpa because Grandpa Shales had built the cottage he once envisioned.

During the summer of 1941, he built the fireplace and chimney with rocks dug out of the nearby shoreline behind Rattan's Point. His youngest brother Elwood, who inherited the family farm, transported the stones across the ice the previous winter on a sled drawn by his Clydesdale workhorses, Ted and Daisy. The following winter Elwood took lumber to the island. Aided by a professional carpenter Grandpa built the cottage in the summer of 1942. The interior room of the non-insulated cottage, warmed by the fireplace in early spring and fall, served as a living room. He equipped the small kitchen with a woodstove, icebox and a hand pump with a water line from the lake. Screened porches on opposite sides of the building served as sleeping and dining areas. Tall pines, hemlock and cedars surrounded the building.

A steep hike over a hill in the centre of the small granite island led to an outhouse, painted dark green and suitably camouflaged by a row of young cedars transplanted by Grandpa. A wooden sign hung on the outside of the door. It said GO in green letters and STOP in red and could be flipped to indicate whether the privy was in use or not. On a nearby slab of granite slanting down to the lake, Grandpa crafted a rock incinerator chimney for burning garbage.

For our second week Uncle Elwood invited us to christen a new cottage on the mainland. Great Uncle Elwood, Grandpa and his two sons had constructed the sturdy log and rough-hewn lumber abode. Named The Cedars, it was the first of five rustic cottages to be built on the shoreline of the family farm. The surrounding grove of tall cedars shaded the interior room, keeping it cool but dark. Mom cooked on the wood stove. She loved the indoor icebox. A large, screened sleeping porch overlooked the narrow beachfront. Spacious and comfortable, The Cedars provided almost all the comforts of home. But it wasn't ours.

The walk through the dark forest to the outhouse frightened me. I imagined wild animals lurking behind every bush. I only went with Mom who had to lift me on to the seat. The unadorned outhouse, a luxurious two-holed palace, exuded an aroma of rough cut pine and cedar. We scurried back inside the cottage, chilled by crisp August breeze from the lake. The flannel sheets layered with red and black wool blankets, Hudson Bay blankets borrowed from Grandma kept us toasty.

Mary beside the Aerie Cottage circa 2021. —Barry Hodgins

Uncle Elwood, the youngest of Grandpa's brothers, had inherited the family farm, 200 hectares bordered on the south by the shore of Draper Lake and extending north to the southern border of Frontenac Provincial Park.

A two-story lakeside cabin called The Aerie was the next build, down the hill from the farmhouse. Elwood and Alice also welcomed summer boarders in spare rooms in the farmhouse left vacant by Elwood's departed siblings. The Cedars and Aerie were originally built for the use of summer sibling visits. Since Harry, the oldest sibling, died after WWII, Jack, William and

Walter built their own cottages and baby Louise married and moved to her husband Arthur Morley's farm. Elwood and Alice soon realized summer rentals on a good fishing lake presented potential income. Once the word was out The Cedars and Aerie were available, week-long bookings to Draper Lake rapidly gained popularity, mostly with American fishermen and their families from the Rochester, New York area. Three other cottages were added in the ensuing years.

Dad said it was time to think about planning for future summers on our own island. "The Cedars is already fully booked for next summer." First Dad had had to convince Mom that camping with three kids on an island she had never set foot on was a good idea.

"We need a place of our own." The screen door of The Cedars cottage slammed behind Dad. "Let's have a look at the island before we have to go back to the city."

He grabbed an empty pail and headed to the lake.

The next afternoon I sat on the patchy grass with Mom watching Donna, Doug, and our second cousin Mary, wading through tall, thin reeds, catching frogs. The coarse dark sand skirting the shallow water, while not as luxurious as the white sands of Bruce Beach, helped Mom feel at home. I dug my red plastic shovel into the sand, filled my pail and dumped it over, creating a village of cylindrical houses. We stayed outside all day.

After dinner Dad built a campfire on the beach. Mom sang gospel tunes. The silhouette of our island, our future summer home, faded in the orange glow of sunset.

Dad pulled Mom close. "We could be out there, all on our own."

I wasn't sure if I was scared, excited, or both.

The winter in Toronto suburbia seemed endless. Donna went off to Grade One and Doug to Grade Two. Left at home with Mom, I crayoned murals on the living room wall and made forts with old blankets draped over the dining room table.

At lunchtime Doug and Donna ran all the way home from Weston's Memorial Public School to not miss Byng Whitteker hosting *The Small Types Club* or Bert Pearl with *The Happy Gang* on our crackling Westinghouse Radio.

Dad toiled at a desk all day at The Canada Life Assurance

Mom aka the Beach Girl at Bruce Beach circa late 30's. —Doug Gordon

Company in downtown Toronto. On weekends he squared off a low enclosure in the back yard with scrap lumber. Long evenings standing in the dark with chilly fingers and frigid toes he created a backyard skating rink. I took my first slippery strides, desperately gripping Mom's hand, bob skates strapped to my boots. On weekends I helped Doug and Donna build snow forts. We staged epic snowball wars against neighbourhood kids. After school Doug dragged me on the family toboggan, wedged between stacks of the Toronto Telegram, while he delivered papers to our neighbours.

Christmas came and went. Mom spent spring days polishing the hardwood floors and doing laundry in the ringer washer in the basement. She hummed Dinah Shore's "Buttons and Bows" as she sashayed around the dining room in a frilly apron over her cotton housedress. She set the dining room table early, made sure dinner was ready and the newspaper remained untouched for Dad's 5 p.m. arrival home from the office.

Iris and tulips bloomed along the backyard fence line. Mom planted a vegetable garden. Then one night over dinner that winter after Mom's first steps on the island Dad talked about escaping the city for his holidays.

"We can stay with Grandma and Grandpa while we set up camp. It will be fun, you'll see." Mom responded with a brave smile.

Then, one afternoon in early July Mom handed me a brown paper grocery bag, the kind with handles. "You can take your teddy bear and whatever other toys you can fit in the bag."

The next morning Mom and Dad loaded the car. We piled in, a typical post-war family with Baby Boomer children, off on an adventure. I kept my shopping bag close to my feet. Dad turned the key in the ignition. The car rumbled to life for the 300 kilometere journey. Only five and a half hours separated us from our first camping adventure on Loon Island.

CHAPTER 2
FOUND IN A CANDY BOX

July 30, 2011

"Look what I found." Doug walks out of the kitchen and places a small rectangular box on my lap. The faded print on the top reads "OLD TIME – HOME MADE Laura Secord CANDIES. "I found it when I was going through things in Dad's apartment." I lift the tattered lid to unveil a back and white photo of our family in Miss Niagara the day of our first official visit to what would become our summer haven.

Barry and I, Donna and her husband Art, and a few of Doug's grandchildren and great grandchildren sit lounging on easy chairs in the living room of the island cottage Doug inherited from our grandparents, Will and Spray. It's happy hour. Doug fetches a chilled bottle of white wine from the refrigerator and wanders around the living room filling glasses for the adults.

"Juice, boiled lake or bottled water," he asks Barry, the non-drinker, and the younger family members.

From the living room we have a clear view of his wife Margo labouring over her specialty garlic-crusted salmon in celebration of Doug's 70th birthday. She slides it in the electric oven, then stands by the counter surveying the crowd.

Doug and Margo have transformed the once dark, chopped-up cottage into one bright, open-plan expanse, giving new respect to the grand rock fireplace and ceiling-high chimney. White pine now covers walls darkened with age and soot. Windows replace screens in the dining porch, extending the season for family gatherings.

While others chat, I sort through the stack of photos. There on the bottom I find myself. The feeling of cool afternoon shade returns me to that first visit to Grandma and Grandpa's cottage. I'm standing in the sandbox behind the cottage, at two years old inexplicably clean in a white cotton dress with what I remember as red hand-embroidered smocking stitch. It must have been taken just weeks before our first visit to our island. Doug looks over my shoulder at my find.

"That sandbox has stood the test of time and generations of Shales. Let's hope it will long after we're gone," Doug says.

We exchange wistful glances with Donna who sits on the other side of me, three retired teachers lost in memories of island summers.

"Lucky Grandpa made that deal with Clarence Stoness. Even if the guys from the Department of Lands and Forest gave Mom and Dad so much grief over whether it was legal or not, it gave our family a foot in the door," I say.

CHAPTER 3
SPLIT LOGS AND
THE SPITTING ROCK

Late August 1949

Tenting Tonight on the Old Camp Ground
We're tenting tonight on the old camp ground,
Give us a song to cheer
Our weary hearts, a song of home
And friends we love so dear.

Walter Kittredge 1864 from the American Civil War
Pale yellow morning rays edged a path across the roof of the
tent, then slipped between the flaps. I opened my eyes. Canvas
dust danced in the light. Overhead an Eastern Phoebe chirped
a cheerful wake up call. Even though it looked like a sunny
day, I felt sad. School started next week. That meant Donna
and Doug would go back to school and Dad would go back to
work. I would be left alone at home with Mom. Today was our
last full day at the lake.

Directly above my head, high on the roof of the tent I noticed
a brown dock spider. My body stiffened. Then I raised my arm
above my face to block my view of the hairy intruder. The
spider looked bigger than my hand. Even with my fingers
stretched out as far as they could go, I could still see it. The
damp, grey, canvas walls of our army surplus tent, worn almost
see-through with age, provided a perfect haven for spiders. It
paused a moment, then continued its journey, picking its way

across our ceiling in search of a meal of mosquitoes and flies. I lay frozen, lips tightly closed, afraid to move or speak in case the spider dropped into my open mouth. I nudged Donna, cuddled beside me, and pointed to the roof.

She jostled Doug, next in line, sleeping sideways on the double camp mattress. I pulled the rough wool of the Hudson's Bay blanket over my head, Doug jumped up, grabbed the fly swatter and attacked the spider.

Donna stretched out her arm and swatted him. "Don't do that. You'll make it rain."

"No, I won't. I missed anyhow." Before he could wind up for another shot the spider plopped down onto the blanket and scurried away through the crack between the worn barn boards of the tent floor.

"Keep it down to a dull roar. Too early." Dad rolled over on the mattress beside us where he was sprawled out with Mom. Sleepily Dad mumbled something about the culprit on the tent ceiling being a fishing spider.

"It lives near the water, like us. Don't worry. It's harmless."

I believed him but still flinched every time one hovered directly above my mouth.

This was the second-last day of Dad's three-week holiday from the Canada Life Assurance Company. One more night and we'd be back in our house on Boyd Avenue in the town of Weston, our neighbourhood in the suburbs of Toronto.

We scrambled out of the tent, eager to make the most of one last day of frog hunting, fishing and swimming.

"Hope the sun lasts all day." Unfazed by the spider, Mom yanked the tent flaps aside and tied them up to the poles to air the dampness out of the packed-cotton mattresses. She draped the sheets and blankets over the nearby clothesline strung between two cedar trees.

"This bedding could do with a good airing before our last night. I'll give it a thorough tumble in the wringer washer when we're back in the city. No more laundry in the lake for this year."

Even with the bedding spread out, loads of room remained on the clothesline. We didn't need many clothes at the lake. We were each allowed one pair of long pants, one long-sleeved shirt, two T-shirts, one pair of shorts, and one set of pyjamas. We also had two pair of underwear, which often doubled as a bathing suit and two pair of socks, which we avoided wearing whenever possible. We stuffed them into our own cardboard box in the tent. Dad considered a sensible pair of lace up running shoes a must for walking into the woods. Around the campsite, the swamp and the swimming rock we kids preferred to go barefoot. The soles of our feet grew calloused by the granite. The cool forest soil cushioned with layers of cedar and pine needles kept them cool.

We sat in a row on the split log bench facing the lake. Mom opened the last can of Donald Duck orange juice and poured some into our plastic camp cups. Dad had fashioned our rustic dining table by laying rows of thin cedar poles across a couple

Loon Island Tent site 1948. —Will Shales

of boards supported by log stumps. The horizontal poles squeezed close together, but remained rounded on top.

"Don't put your juice down like that." Doug caught my glass just before it spilled. I didn't like it when he was so bossy.

"I want the Rice Krispies," I blurted out.

Mom pulled the Kellogg's Variety Pack out from under the lid of one of the galvanized metal tubs used to protect our food from animals. I remembered to call out to beat Doug to first choice today. Mom grabbed a paring knife. I watched her cut slits along the dotted line to open each individual serving box. Rice Krispies for me.

Dad poured milk into my box. I turned my head, one ear down to the box.

"Snap, crackle and pop."

"Shut up, Pretzl." Doug said, using the nickname he knew I hated. He was mad I had called out first choice.

Breakfast over, Doug and Donna hunted frogs among the cattails in the swampy area for a while.

"Go for the green leopard frogs. They're best for catching bass," Doug said, in his usual instructive big brother, seasoned fisherman tone. They caught two frogs each, stuffed them in an old juice can, covered it with a wet rag and disappeared behind the tent to retrieve their bamboo fishing poles. Dad had tied fishing line to the narrow end of each ten-foot pole. Each line had a small lead weight - we called them sinkers - near the end of the line, and a single hook. Doug helped Donna put a live frog on her hook, then ruthlessly impaled his own. They splashed through the swamp to the shallows at one end of the swimming rock. The tips of the poles reached out past the drop-off to the deep water. In the clear water off the rock schools of sunfish, rock bass, small and large mouthed bass and perch frolicked every which way, scales flashing in the sun. Deeper, in the darker water the occasional catfish lurked.

I was happy on higher ground. The only time I'd be willing to wade through the ankle-deep water of the swamp was for swim time. Then I'd dash through, shoulders high, petrified I might step on a black rat snake.

A few hours later Dad started toward the path into the woods. "Let's get some wood for a campfire," he said. I followed through dense cedars taller than my head. I loved having Dad all to myself.

"Here you are. An acorn. It'll be a grand oak tree one day."

A bit farther along he pushed aside a moldy leaf with the toe of his shoe to find a creamy white snail shell. "I wonder who used to live in there. I bet his shell was as brown as the dirt before he moved out."

I learned to tell a pine from a hemlock, a maple from an oak and the look of the marks a beaver's teeth left on a birch stump.

Tenting campfire rock. —Patti Shales Lefkos

Dad pointed out poison ivy as he did hundreds of times in the years to come. I leaned down for a closer look.

"One stem with three dark shiny leaves. Don't touch." I looked hard but never learned to tell the difference from so many other small green plants in the underbrush. My feet developed the rhythm needed for stepping over roots. The crunch of pinecones and snapping of twigs added staccato to our wanderings.

Dad stepped off the path and picked up some dead branches.

"Hold your arms out front." He placed a pile of twigs across my outstretched arms.

"You can help by carrying firewood to Mom. We need a small fire. It's coffee time." He grabbed an armful of larger pieces and led the way as we retraced our steps along the path, soft underfoot with seasons of fallen leaves.

Back at the tent site he built a small teepee of twigs under the fire grate situated in a damp area near the edge of the marsh. The large rock behind the fire acted as a windbreak. Once the fire flared Mom settled a saucepan full of lake water on the grate to boil for washing the breakfast dishes.

"How about a cup of coffee?"

Mom produced a brown jar of Nescafe Instant and two heavy cream-coloured mugs. Over the years Dad loved to regale us with the story of how these mugs suspiciously went missing when he and Uncle Dave abandoned their jobs as teenaged canoe guides at Camp Franklin on Georgian Bay, the northwestern arm of Lake Huron near Parry Sound, Ontario. "They asked us to bury a dead horse. They had left it out in the sun too many days. So we left. The cook donated a few necessary provisions: oatmeal for porridge, coffee and a couple of Camp Franklin mugs, bowls and plates." They'd had enough of camp life. Instead of going home to London, Ontario, they made their way, using only a road map, via various waterways, to Draper Lake. "We loaded Miss Niagara and paddled home to Draper Lake via Georgian Bay, the Trent

Canal system and along the shore of Lake Ontario. We'd pull Miss Niagara up on the shore and sleep underneath." Coffee mixed, Mom and Dad settled on the bench. Dad helped me up. I snuggled in beside him.

Donna and Doug soon tired of fishing by mid-afternoon. It

Granite front swimming rock. —Patti Shales Lefkos

was swim time. Mom helped me out of my T-shirt and shorts. Donna and Doug slipped out of theirs and laid them on the rock beside their fishing poles. All three of us swam in cotton undies.

"There's no one else on the lake but Grandma and Grandpa. So who cares? Besides I want your bathing suits dry when I pack them," Mom said.

"Okay, Trish. Time to show me your swimming."

Only Dad called me Trish. It felt special. Our secret.

I gathered courage to follow Dad through the marsh. Black mush squirted up between my toes. I sprinted, eyes peeled for snakes, and made it to the swimming rock unscathed.

"I'll stand on the edge of the drop-off. You swim around me."

"Can I just hold on to one of your hands?"

"You don't need to do that anymore. You'll swim better using both hands."

I peered off into the deep emerald water by his toes. He stood waist-deep, toes curled around on the edge of the rock drop off. One frantic deep breath and I set off in a furious dog paddle, legs churning like an eggbeater. I stretched my neck, struggling to keep my chin above the surface. Gasping, I stayed afloat almost all the way around Dad. Dad grabbed me just before I completed the semi-circle. My toes searched frantically for the stability of the familiar rock. Finally I stood triumphant, up to my neck, beside dad.

"I knew you could do it."

"I want to go again."

I knew this was one of my last chances to practice. Doug and Donna executed smooth shallow dives off the rock and splashed each other like sleek otter pups. Already strong swimmers at aged nine and eight they had earned the privilege of going out in the rowboat by themselves. I wanted to be just like them. Dad patiently hovered at the drop-off for two more rounds. Then he lifted me high, turned and placed me in the shallow water. "My turn. Stay there."

I watched as he pushed off in a Johhny Weissmuller – Tarzan-

Marl beach. —Patti Shales Lefkos

style front crawl, muscled arms glistening in the sun, toward Grandpa and Grandma's island. A few minutes later Mom joined him, her powerful strokes matching his. I watched from the Front Rock.

After lunch Mom made us take a nap. She said an hour. It seemed to drag on forever. We lounged side by side in the shade on towels.

Mom and Dad sauntered back to the tent and closed the flaps. They told us it was because of the mosquitoes. I wondered what they were doing in there. Finally they emerged, relaxed and smiling, nap time over.

For the next few hours we settled on the limestone marl beach on the grassy edge of the swamp. An earthy mixture of fine-grained materials, the sediment forms limestone, under pressure, over time. We dug down with spoons and our one cracked plastic shovel below the layer of tiny snail shell carapaces, most ground beyond recognition to form a fine marl.

"I found a good one. Look."

I held up the tiny undamaged shell, smaller than the end of my pinky finger, for Donna to inspect.

With tarnished soup spoons we filled empty cans and egg cups, then upturned them to construct an entire village of houses, a school and a church. Lines of pebbles defined roads, ferns and twigs delineated tree-lined walkways.

Underneath the layer of marl we discovered sticky gray clay.

"Let's make bowls." We dampened the clay, smoothed layer after layer on the upturned camp bowls and left them to dry in the sun.

Mom lifeguarded our afternoon swim from her position on a tattered towel placed on the rock to protect her skirted blue bathing suit. "Sit here, with me." She placed a gray enamel bowl of vegetables fresh from Grandpa's section of garden at the farm beside her. The rhythmic buzz of Dad's crosscut saw sounded from the woods behind us where he worked to fell cedars to clear a site for our future cottage.

Doug and Donna swam out toward Grandpa's island.

"Don't go too far from shore."

She turned to me.

"Okay, you can go in now."

Restricted to the shallow water right in front of her, I paddled around on my stomach, pretending to swim. Most of the time my hands reached the bottom.

Soon chilled, I rejoined her, bottom warmed by the rock. A blackened cooking pot balanced between us.

"You can help me shell the peas. Here, into the pot, like this." With skilled precision she slit each pea pod with her thumbnail. Strong freckled hands on autopilot, her eyes never wandered from the swimmers.

"Watch this dive Mom. Are my legs straight?"

"Look at my front crawl. Is it getting better?"

"Yes, I saw it. Almost straight that time. Try to breathe every second stroke. Just count one, two."

By 4 p.m., shortly before the sun ducked behind the island, she'd had enough sun and humidity. "Okay. That's it. I can't stand the heat. My turn. Everybody out of the water." She strode down the granite ramp into the shallows, dove into the deep, turned on her back and floated, gazing up at the clouds.

Refreshed, she rotated her torso and alternately stretched out tanned arms to execute a perfect Esther Williams circle crawl, smoothly turning her body, barely rippling the surface. Back at the rock she stood in the shallows, unsnapped the chinstrap of her white bathing cap to display now tousled ash-blond hair.

"That's how it's done."

Our last dinner unfolded uneventfully, featuring fresh peas with canned beef stew and canned white potatoes, both dished out of iconic red Aylmer brand tins heated over the campfire. For dessert, a special treat. Earlier in the day Grandpa had dropped off a small basket of raspberries from Aunt Alice's garden. Mom poured a miserly drizzle of maple syrup from Uncle Elwood's sugar bush over each mound of raspberries. "I'm saving the last bit for porridge tomorrow. The cereals are all gone." Porridge for breakfast was a sure sign of fall. Time to go back to the city.

After dinner Dad loaded a bucket of empty cans and bottles into the green boat. Donna jumped in and sat in the back seat, Doug at the oars.

"Can I go, too?" I said.

"I guess so. The rowboat's pretty stable."

I sat in the middle seat, siblings close by.

"Don't stand up in the boat, any of you. And stay out front."

Dad pushed us off. Doug rowed us out over the deep water about half way over to Grandpa's island. One by one our hands released the cans and bottles over the edge of the boat. We watched in fascination as they twirled into the depths, finally disappearing into the darkness.

By 8:00 p.m. we'd gathered outside the tent, already in pyjamas, for the nightly ritual.

"Stand back." We immediately withdrew into the shadows

of the forest, well back from Dad who was wielding the DDT sprayer like the weapon it turned out to be. Our health-conscious parents had no idea that DDT, developed in the 1940s to combat insect-borne diseases, would later be banned.

Mom handed us each a plastic cup. "Go fill up at the washstand. Come back for a squirt of toothpaste."

Beside the tent, well into the woods, a large flat pointed rock jutted out like the prow of a ship over an expansive dip in the ground. Mom and Dad had designated this granite protrusion as a safe place to brush teeth and to dump water from washing dishes. At least some of our routines respected the environment. There was only room for one of us at a time to stand at the high point.

"First on the rock."

Doug raced to the washstand, filled his cup from the water pail and sprinted back. Victorious, he stepped onto The Spitting Rock. Donna was up second. I was third, as usual. We brushed, then spit with as much force as possible to see who could splatter toothpaste the farthest on to the forest floor. Competition over for the last time that summer; Mom frowned on indoor spitting competitions. Doug declared himself the winner.

Mom switched on her flashlight, held it high to light the path behind her and led Donna and me into the woods for a visit to The Split Log, our family latrine. Dad had dug a rectangular hole, one metre by 30 cm, about 60 cm deep in one of the few areas with ample soil. He constructed an open-air biffy with a split log, rounded side up, halves placed about 20 cm apart, just enough span for the comfort of a medium sized derriere. Two parallel split logs atop four cedar poles. A rung halfway down provided a spot to rest your feet on at the front. In my case it sometimes had to act as a ladder. Stabilized, somewhat precariously, by cedar poles set in triangular formation, it accommodated two contributors at a time. Mom lifted and placed me on top and handed me a wad of toilet paper kept dry in the tent. In constant fear of falling off, or worse, into the middle, I clutched the log on either side of me. Concentration on the purpose at hand was often close to impossible.

Dad and Doug peed in the bushes. We congregated outside the tent for the evening rush through the lingering veil of DDT. A few mosquitoes got in but didn't bother me.

"OK. Hold your breath. Plug your nose. Go." Once inside, Mum tucked us in. Almost asleep we heard the plaintive call of a raft of loons.

"They congregate at the end of August. They're getting ready to go south for the winter. They'll be back. So will we," Dad said.

From the dawn call of the phoebe to the good night sounds of the loons, the sounds of the island encircled our summer story.

CHAPTER 4
POISON IVY

July 1995

*N*o one expected anything out of the ordinary. Family members hunkered down for the night in their individual Draper Lake cottages on the eve of Bastille Day, July 14, France's national holiday. Barry and I slipped into our tent on our building site on the northeast of Loon Island. After what happened next, it's safe to say we won't easily forget. When the derecho, defined as a straight-line windstorm associated with severe thunderstorms, blasted Loon Island around midnight, Barry and I were asleep, al fresco, in our tent at the base of our one-room bunkie building site. I woke up abruptly to what sounded like a freight train careening through our tent. Instantly soaked, the tent walls imploded around us in the 180 km winds. We fought our way out of the sagging nylon and headed for cover in Mom and Dad's cottage on the other side of the island. Part way along Barry stopped me.

"Don't go like that. You'll frighten your parents."

Barry ran back to the tent to get clothes and shoes for us. Still nude, shivering violently in shock, but ever the well-trained outdoor girl, I scrunched down, wrapped in a towel, to conserve body heat. Barry returned. We dressed hurriedly in the rain, clothes whipped by the wind.

In only a few minutes more than one hundred trees had fallen every which way, like pieces in a game of Pick-up Sticks, uprooted from the thin soil of the Canadian Shield. Gale force winds downed a huge pine tree right next to Donna's cottage. Its roots,

which reached under the cabin floor almost wrenched the build-
ing off its foundation. The branch of a large pine punched through
Doug's cottage roof then came to rest on a soaked and sagging hy-
dro line. A trio of mature, majestic white birches slammed down
inches from our tent. Three towering pines crashed onto the back
of the bedroom roof at Mom and Dad's cottage, blasting out the
plate glass of their bedroom's front window.

Making our way through leafy crowns of felled trees, glass
crackling underfoot, we reached the family cottage. All three of
us, Doug,55, Donna, 54 and me, 50, with our spouses, returned
to home base, to console our collective shock, plan cleanup and
restoration. Dad, just turned eighty, was the first to climb a
ladder and inspect his roof at dawn the next morning.

"I guess I'd better go to the walk in clinic in Kingston. I can't sit
down and I can't stand the itching any more," I said. Barry looked
over to witness my aggravated expression.

"I thought you said you never get poison ivy."

"I never have before. Guess I should have paid more attention to
Dad's bush lessons when I was little. Turns out scrunching down
in the wet woods to conserve body heat wasn't such a good idea."

It wasn't until 1985 while studying for a Masters Degree in
Environmental Education at Simon Fraser University in BC,
that I realized how much of my deeply held appreciation of the
environment had originated from summers spent with Dad on
our island. Even though we sank cans and bottles in the lake,
common practice in those days, our family developed a profound
feeling sense of respect, almost a worship of our island sanctuary
and surrounding water. Draper Lake was said to be one hundred
feet deep. Surely, we reasoned, it could hide a few cans and bottles.
And, it was spring fed with several outlet creeks, so the water
circulated. Besides, only Uncle Elwood, Aunt Alice and Mary and

one other farm family lived on the lakeshore full time. Foolishly oblivious, we proceeded this way for several more years, unaware of the damage to the environment, until around the time we realized that using DDT wasn't such a good idea either.

CHAPTER 5
WHAT DO YOU MEAN WE DON'T OWN THE ISLAND?

August 1949

One incident during that same summer of 1949 when I turned three, cemented my ambition and determination to learn to swim as confidently as my siblings.

Mom paced back and forth a few times then returned to the outdoor dining table from her third walk out to the end of the dock. She tugged Dad's old plaid shirt she was wearing close to her body with arms tightly folded against the blustering August wind.

"Where are those kids? No sight of them from the end of the dock."

Dad, engrossed in a Zane Grey novel, looked up.

"Better go look for them." He stood, stretched and grabbed a canoe paddle from its place leaning on a tree.

"The storm's about to get worse. That old motor on the rowboat is in terrible shape. I'm surprised it works at all."

I begged to go with him, tired of always being left behind. "Please. I never get to go anywhere."

Dad hesitated, looked out at the lake, then succumbed to my whine. I trailed after him. He steadied the canoe next to the simple catwalk dock he had slapped together from used lumber at the first of the summer.

"One hand on each side." Dad said.

I stretched my arms and placed one hand on each gunwale.

Family in green rowboat ready for an outing on a calm day. —Will Shales

Dad reminded me every time we went in the canoe. I stepped in and sat in the bottom, facing front.

"Sit still," said Dad. "You know the rule. If the canoe tips, hang on to the boat. Never leave the boat." He pushed off with one toe, settled in on his knees, and with a few strong strokes faced us directly into the wind toward the end of the island. Mom watched from shore, her forehead wrinkled in concern.

Donna and Doug, competent swimmers, prided themselves in their independent status. They were allowed to venture off island on their own. We didn't own any lifejackets. Dad deemed the only lifejackets available, the WWII navy lifejackets, too orange, too bulky and way too uncomfortable.

"It's safer to learn to swim on your own, without one. You can't depend on a lifejacket. Your head could slip through the hole and then where would you be?"

Just three years old I was allowed to venture into the deep water but only with my inflatable green and white plastic water wings. With the colourful balloons clutched across my chest and secured under my arms I could almost keep up with my siblings. Without them I could only stay afloat for a few strokes in the shallows.

Every time Donna and Doug rowed away from dock or took Miss Niagara out for a spin, Dad reminded them of the rules he preached as a canoe guide. That gusty afternoon his words came back to haunt him.

Right after lunch Doug and Donna had been sent on an errand to the farm to fetch a block of ice from Uncle Elwood's icehouse. They motored off in the four-metre-long green rowboat. A mail-order vessel from a catalogue, it had arrived early that summer by train from the T. Eaton Company in Toronto. Dad went with Uncle Elwood to pick it up at the tiny Perth Road Village station. Uncle Elwood helped Dad remove the cardboard packing and immediately noticed daylight shining between the floorboards. He took a step back.

"That boat will never last."

How wrong he was. Admittedly, there were exciting times early on when rapid bailing was required.

Over the years Dad repeatedly sealed the seams with pine tar and eventually replaced most of the gaping floorboards. Flat bottomed, it was a safe, stable boat for Doug and Donna to use for fishing expeditions and errands.

Earlier that day, Mom had returned from the icebox behind the tent. Strapped to a tree for stability on the uneven ground, the second-hand treasure had replaced Dad's former hole in-ground cooling system.

"That last ice block has almost melted. It won't last much longer. I don't want the milk to spoil."

Mom poured milk into her tea and then some for Dad.

"Time for the kids to go to the farm for ice. Better go now while the weather holds."

The icehouse stood a short walk up the hill from the lake next to the family farmhouse. An upper floor of the drive shed provided summer storage for ice blocks cut out of the lake the previous winter. Farm ice was the closest available source and by far the cheapest.

"Here, take this quarter to give to Elwood. And don't forget the ice-tongs."

With each of them holding the handle on either side of the tongs they could manage to carry the block down the hill from the farm and heave it into the flat bottom of the rowboat.

Doug had been keen all day for another try with the ancient outboard engine gifted to him by Grandma's brother, our Great Uncle Orie. The tiny motor barely propelled the green rowboat in barge-like fashion.

Cousin Mary met Doug and Donna at the top of the hill and led them up the ladder past the rain blackened boards of the decades-old building. They squealed with shivers when their bare toes slipped through the sawdust layers to contact the ice. Mary used a hatchet to free a 30 cm square block and removed it from the row of blocks with a set of tongs. With muscled arms she flung it out the window to the ground.

Donna grasped one side of our ice tongs, Doug the other. Somehow they managed, with several rest periods to catch green grasshoppers for fishing bait, to wrestle the weighty block down the hill and into the rowboat.

Angry clouds darkened the horizon. Just out of sight around the tip of the island from our dock Dad and I finally found Doug and Donna. The spindly one-horse motor coughed and sputtered. Then it died. Waves rocked the rowboat.

"I can't get it started," Doug said.

Blasting winds almost obliterated Doug's words. His expression stormed as dark as the sinister sky. Donna's arms strained against the whitecaps. She hauled on the water-logged oars, trying her best to make progress.

"It's too windy. I can't pull hard enough," Donna said, eyes glistening.

Dad paddled closer to offer advice. The waves broadsided us, careening the canoe dangerously close to the rowboat. He braced Miss Niagara with his paddle against the vertical wooden side of the green rowboat.

"Never push off from another boat with your paddle." Dad had repeated that rule often enough. I was about to witness why.

The two boats rocked closer together. As Dad finished talking, he pushed off from the rowboat with his paddle. It slipped. Just as he had always said it would. Over we went. I splashed into the lake, arms flailing, sputtering mouthfuls of lake. Before I realized what was happening and before I had time to be frightened, I felt Dad's arms around me.

Seconds later, I lay wet and shivering across the upturned hull of Miss Niagara. My shivering fingers struggled to grip the slippery keel. With one hand on the upturned canoe and one on my back, Dad kicked furiously, pushing the canoe back the ten-metre distance to the dock while I sprawled face down on top, clutching the keel to keep from slipping off. When we reached shore he handed me up to Mom. In what seemed only a moment I was wrapped in the warmth of Mom's plaid shirt.

"Well, that's your afternoon swim for the day." Mom tried to make a joke of it. She wasn't about to pamper me over a little unexpected dunking. She thought fawning over me might make me afraid of travelling in our boats. Not a good thing for an island dweller.

Tears exploded from my eyes at the idea of missing a chance to practice my swimming and play with my water wings. Even more upsetting than being unceremoniously dumped was the state of my footwear. I squished and stomped my way from the dock through the swamp to the Front Rock and sat down if a huff on the warm granite.

Sun peeked through the clouds. We heard a noise. Doug finally got the motor going. I heard the sputter of Uncle Orie's decrepit engine as Donna and Doug returned safely to the dock. Tired of being left behind when Doug and Donna disappeared on grand adventures, I was more determined than ever to learn to swim in the black water all by myself. Ominous clouds had dispersed as rapidly as they gathered. Heartbroken but hopeful, I removed my new red sandals and arranged them facing the sun. Head on my knees, I sat down, wrapped myself in a towel and waited for swim time. Doug and Donna joined me on the rock. When they realized I was fine they went to change into their bathing suits.

Mom dutifully assumed her lifeguard position. I waded in until the water reached my chest, lay face down and proceeded to dog paddle my way to the shallow end of the rock and back again, over and over, until my lips turned blue. Mom finally had to drag me out of the water to get me warmed up and changed for dinner. Our parents didn't make a big deal out of the incident so we didn't either. I never developed a fear of a canoe tipping unexpectedly or things going amiss during a distance swim.

By the end of July I had gained the privilege of venturing close to the drop off during practice sessions with Dad, edging ever closer to the black water.

Back in Toronto sometime during the following winter, a threatening letter arrived from the Department of Lands and Forests. The letter, questioning our family's ownership of Loon Island, ignited Dad's long, drawn-out correspondence with a raft of faceless bureaucrats then based in Tweed, Ontario. A precursor to the Ministry of Natural Resources, the Department had the audacity to question the authenticity of the quit claim procedure with which Grandpa had purchased our island. First they queried whether island properties could even considered to be owned by the farmer who holds the deed to the adjacent land, even if the islands are within his concession's boundaries. They claimed Clarence Stoness, deemed the owner and grantor of the island properties, had never properly registered the original decades old sale to the grantee, my grandfather.

Mom and Dad did their best to laugh off the outrageous claims. I didn't fully understand what the letters meant but I was old enough at three and a half to sense the gloom and tension that accompanied this official missive. Grim faced, Dad wrote back. Lands and Forest disagreed. With each ensuing letter Dad disappeared to his desk in the master bedroom to compose a response that would fend them off a while longer.

One Sunday evening Mom and Dad gathered us in front of the log fireplace. Mom passed around our Sunday night treat, cheesies, small squares of whole wheat bread topped with melted cheese and bacon, toasted on long metal forks over the open fire. This supper made us think of the island. It was like any other Sunday night in the city, until Dad's tone got serious.

"We have something to tell you. The boys at the Lands and Forests office are trying to tell us we don't own the island."

"But it's our island," we shouted, almost in unison. We couldn't imagine how some strangers in a office somewhere had the nerve to question a fact so obvious.

"They won't try to take it away, will they?" Donna said.

"Don't worry. I'll write another letter." Dad's dark expression morphed from one of despair to a devilish grin.

"They won't do anything until they can prove it. I'll just keep writing letters and we'll keep going to the island. I can keep this going for years." Mom stared into the fire.

Mom tucked me in first. At some point during the night I woke up to hear whispers drifting from Mom and Dad's bedroom next to mine.

"I don't know if we'll be able to manage it." That, in Dad's low voice followed by a long bout of silence.

"We have to. The kids will be so disappointed if we don't. Besides, we know the island's rightfully ours." This, from the Beach Girl who had somehow become at home in the forest.

I lay still. Afraid to breathe. I could make out words like mortgage and salary. I had no idea what they meant. But they didn't sound happy.

CHAPTER 6
WHITECAPS

July 2016

"*It's amazing we're made it this far,*" *I chuckle, somewhat breathlessly.*

I haul on the oars of Grandpa's seventy-two-year-old red rowboat. My preferred mode of transportation, two years older than me, it still dances lightly on the choppy water. The waves slam the boat broadside. My niece Sherri, one of Donna's four daughters, faces me in the stern. She and her husband Paul are here for their annual week-long visit, staying in our original family cottage. Sherri comes to visit with her cousins. Paul plays golf at the nearby course outside Inverary village. We're on the way back to Loon Island from a social visit to Turkey Island, now owned by her cousin Drue, Doug's daughter. Sherri's knuckles have turned white from gripping the sides of the dancing boat for stabilty. We rock sideways, bouncing through the peaks and troughs. Frothy whitecaps chop the surface. Sherri's hair gusts sideways, a flash of red and gold in the afternoon sun. As we round the tip of our island she looks sideways.

"*Look out. We're going to hit that rock.*"

She rolls up one leg of her shorts. With the grace and strength of the professional dancer she once was, she extends her leg outside the boat, contacts the flat rock with one foot and pushes us safely away.

"*Okay, Auntie P. Over to you. Go for it.*"

I row well, despite my age. My arms ache with the effort. With one more forceful pull we're blown free of the rock.

Patti rowing Grandpa's rowboat on a calmer day. —Barry Hodgins

"*Great job. This is hilarious. I've never seen the waves so high.*"

We both find the adventure fun and exhilarating, secure in the knowledge we could easily swim to any family island in the unlikely event that Grandpa's sturdy rowboat swamped. Members of the Shales clan maintain the fierce resilience of their ancestors. Several generations, we each share an intimate, unwavering connection to the farmland, islands and lake. Still no lifejackets in sight, except for waterskiing; we have all been raised to swim with strength and confidence.

"*Oh, I've seen the waves this high. Even higher. This reminds me of the day I got dumped out of the canoe when I was little. It turned out to be an exciting day for your mom and Uncle Doug, too.*"

A few more solid pulls and the wind pushes toward my dock. With practiced hands we secure the boat.

"*What? You've never heard that story? Time for a cup of tea?*"

CHAPTER 7
HOW MANY MILES?

Early July 1951

"How many miles?"

It seemed we'd been stuck in the car forever. The skin of my short bare legs glued itself to the seat plastic of our 1946 two-tone gray Chevrolet Stylemaster.

We got the car from our Grandpa Gordon, Mom's dad. It was already five years old, so Grandpa gave us a great deal. "We're lucky to have a car at all," Dad always said.

Donna glared in my direction. "You've asked the same thing about ten times." She sounded as if she'd had enough of that question. She was sitting on the right side of the back seat. I was perched on the left, Mom squished between us. Petite at five foot two, her feet rested perfectly on the hump in the middle of the floor. Dad loomed tall in the driver's seat, blocking my view. Beside him, Doug shared space with our new collie puppy, Roger.

I thought Roger looked just like Lassie, the canine star of television and movies. I got to choose his name. I'm not sure if it was because I was the youngest or because I blurted out my choice first when Dad asked, "What will we call him?" I adored cowboy comics. I regularly raided Doug's stash to look at the pictures. I dreamt of riding the range with my six-gun heroes Hopalong Cassidy, Gene Autry and Roy Rogers. I was rarely without my red handled six-gun slung around my hips in a leather holster. I practiced my cross draw for hours. So it's no surprise that before anyone else could speak I announced his name would be Roy Rogers. "How about Roger?" Dad said, and that was that.

Mom insisted on the seating arrangement. She hoped it would keep the peace on the long drive. Doug constantly teased and tickled us if he sat in the back. Then Donna and I would complain. Secretly we knew he would be there to protect us if any of the bigger boys in our neighbourhood ever gave us any trouble.

I had loved kindergarten. Turned out I was pretty good at the colouring, cutting and pasting, singing the songs and memorizing poems Miss Lawrence taught us at Memorial Public School in Weston, our suburban town. But I was glad it was over if it meant going to the lake. I didn't see much of Donna and Doug in the city. We were in different grades, had different activities. They always had homework to do. On the island it was different. I had them all to myself most of the time. I loved my time with them.

This was the first time we were going the first week of July. I wondered how cold the lake would be. We usually didn't get a chance to swim until mid-summer when Dad took his holidays. Donna and Doug finished Grade 4 with flying colours. Donna skipped a year so they were in the same class, both really smart. Already movie-star handsome, Doug had deep brown eyes and a killer smile. Donna's silky blond natural waves framed her cheeks. Blue eyes like Mom's. I had Dad's hair. Fine for a man, but too curly, too brown, and way too frizzy for a girl especially in the summer humidity.

It felt like we'd been in the car for days. In reality, we had left Weston and headed east along Lake Ontario on Highway 2 only a little more than five hours before. Our one escape from the car was a picnic at the Municipal Park in Port Hope, a town about halfway to Kingston. Mom had made all my favourites, all meticulously wrapped in waxed paper: egg salad sandwiches, celery sticks, radishes cut in rosebuds and chocolate brownies with chocolate icing.

"Almost there," Dad called over his right shoulder after endless games of I Spy With My little Eye as we drove through

Remnants of Charlie Hughson's Perth Road Store 2021. —Patti Shales Lefkos

sleepy Ontario towns. "We'll be at The Corners in a few minutes." He meant Perth Road Village, a drowsy hamlet of five hundred people, about three kilometers from the lake, thirty-two kilometres north of Kingston. Moments later we passed Scullion's General Store in the centre of the village on the right. We didn't usually shop there. The Scullions were Catholic. We belonged to the United Church. In those days, one church or another was a religious and a social hub for many. Besides, the name Scullions alone gave me the willies.

Dad pulled the car over in front of Charlie Hughson's grocery store. Charlie, the postmaster, was Protestant. Grandpa Gordon,

Mom's dad, was a Protestant minister. We regularly attended Westminster United Church in Weston during the winter. Mom crawled across me to get out to pick up some milk. I was hoping for ice cream, or a bottle of Orange Crush but I knew Dad would say, "Maybe next time," so I didn't ask. We were only allowed treats once a week. She slid back in beside me and parked the milk on her lap.

Farther along the road we passed the Catholic church on the left and Perth Road United on the right. A few minutes later Dad took a sharp left turn onto the rough dirt road. Dust rose behind us, gravel crunched under the tires. Grass sprouted between the wheel ruts. The second the tires left the pavement butterflies of anticipation fluttered under my ribcage. Dad's shoulders dropped several centimetres in relaxation. Roger craned his neck to poke his nose out of the triangular vent window relishing the unfamiliar country smells of his first Draper Lake summer. I leaned back for a look up at the canopy of maple and poplar branches entwined over the narrow road. Dappled sun danced across the hood of the car.

Shales Road this way 2021. —Barry Hodgins

About two kilometres later we reached Kellar's Hill, the steep, blind, one-lane incline named for the owner of the adjacent land. I held my breath and made a silent wish we wouldn't meet a car racing at us from the opposite direction. It didn't help when Dad said, "Charlie Hughson drives the mail route like a maniac." We made it over the top unscathed. Safely down the other side I sat up as tall as I could. Seconds later Doug called out, "I can see the lake." I leaned over and forward but Mom blocked me from reaching out to give him a punch in the arm. Doug always got to say it first. With Dad's six foot, two-hundred-pound bulk in front of me there was no way I could compete.

Soon a small cottage appeared under tall pines and bushy maples on the left. Great Uncle Walter and his wife Great Aunt Hazel strolled across their lawn to greet us at their gate when Dad pulled over for a quick chat. Walter, my Grandpa Shales' identical twin brother, wore glasses with thick coke-bottle lenses. That's what made it easy to tell him apart from Grandpa. I felt disappointed for Walt and Hazel. Their cottage was on the lakeshore, reducing them to second-class citizen status, in my book. Camping on an island constituted a far more daring and adventuresome lifestyle.

"Aunt Hazel's wearing sandals with socks." Donna announced, this with a hint of scorn when we were out of earshot. I didn't see anything wrong with that but invariably agreed with my big sister's more worldly views on fashion.

We continued along the narrow dirt road, the perimeter of the lake down a gentle slope on our left and a steep treed incline on our right. The road veered tightly to the right and dipped to a one-lane bridge crossing a slow-moving creek. "Looks like the beavers have dammed the outlet." Dad peered down past the low cement abutment. I sat up straight and strained to see. The rims of the water lilies barely rippled with the current. Dad mumbled to himself, barely audible. "The High Water boys will be happy."

Doug reached down to pat Roger's head. He had slept most of the trip, jumping up only occasionally for new sounds and smells.

"The Front Rock might still be under water," Doug said. Dad and Doug remained silent, both lost in thoughts of a surreptitious pre-dawn canoe trip up the creek to the dam.

"A few sticks mysteriously moved before anyone else is awake will take care of that. No harm done," Dad said, lips curved in a secretive smile.

Spring-fed, from cracks deep in the Canadian Shield granite, a hundred feet under the surface, our lake was cold, clear and drinkable – a perfect haven for fish. Edged by unspoiled rock and natural marshy shoreline it remained as pristine as it had been for centuries. I was looking forward to snagging a green leopard frog and baiting the lone hook at the end of the line on my bamboo pole so I could catch the first bass of the season.

Past the bridge a small white farmhouse nested on the hill rising from a marshy shoreline. Great Uncle Charlie and his wife, Great Aunt Jessie, waved from their vegetable garden. Aunt Jessie's faded blue housedress grazed the tops of the vines as she meandered between the rows, harvesting early beans. I was never sure where they fit into the family tree. But I'd heard Dad say Uncle Charlie was a "hard worker". I rolled my window down a bit lower for a possible whiff of fresh bread.

"You three can row over to Jessie's Bay tomorrow to see if she has done any baking. Nothing like a slice of Jessie's warm bread." I couldn't wait. I loved Aunt Jessie. Too reserved for hugs, her welcome shone in the warmth of her smiling gray eyes.

A few minutes later we passed a towering two-storey Victorian frame farmhouse. The stately edifice was built in 1868 by my Great, Great Grandfather, John Harbor Shales I, the first white person settled on the edge of Draper Lake. At that time his was the only house at the end of the road. He and his wife Mary Thomas arrived from Wisbech, a small market town in Cambridgeshire, England, hoping to eke out a living on the unforgiving scant soil of the Canadian Shield. Still owned by extended family. Today the house exudes a quiet well-cared for grandeur, white with green trim.

"Ready everyone?" I covered my ears. I knew what was coming. Dad blasted the car horn twice, once long, once short. No phones on the islands. One long, one short was our family's arrival signature. The sound blared across the windless surface of the lake, announcing our presence to my grandparents at their island cottage. I strained to sit up higher, hoping to get a glimpse of the lake. Roger offered a gentle woof to add to the air of excitement.

Dad maneuvered the car up a gentle hill, rounded one more bend to reach the end of the road. He pulled onto the side lawn of a second grand white Victorian farmhouse. This one had a splendid view of the lake. William Edward Shales, my grandpa's father, built this house. William Shales, my grandpa, was born in a log cabin where this house now stands.

Dad switched off the ignition, sighed and sat a moment in silence. Then, all hell broke loose. Great Uncle Elwood came roaring around the corner of the house bellowing a welcome.

Approach to Elwood and Alice's farmhouse 2021. —Barry Hodgins

Grandpa's younger brother, Elwood, then in his late fifties, remained as beneficiary of the family farm when his older siblings went off to pursue higher education. The youngest, and only girl, Great Aunt Louise, married local boy Arthur Morley and moved to his nearby farm. Shirtless and sweaty in grimy overalls, Elwood rocketed into the scene, larger than life, big-hearted, boisterous and full of fun. I sidled closer to Mom. Sometimes Elwood's rowdy antics scared me.

His wife, Great Aunt Alice, followed close behind, wiping floured hands on the apron bib stretched across her ample bosom. Her gentle hug smelled like the buns she baked in the wood-fired oven in the farmhouse kitchen. Cousin Mary, aged ten, stood behind her mother, head down in silence. We hadn't seen her all winter. It usually took a few days before we got to know her again.

Doug swung open the creaky passenger door. Roger bolted and raced straight at the farm dog, yapping and nipping at its heels. The older, more mature border collie stood its ground, master of his domain. The two dogs circled and sniffed. Dad stepped out, stretched and opened the trunk. A man of a few words, eager to get to the island, he started unloading and barking orders.

"Don't leave the car empty handed. Everyone carry something." He exchanged brief pleasantries with Elwood while placing boxes on the grass.

"And come back up the hill for another load." We'll have to make a few trips each up and down the hill to the lake. All I wanted to do is rush down the hill to look for frogs and turtles.

Winters in a Toronto suburb seemed like a waiting room for island summers. Our family haven was a utopia of scraggly cedars, stately pines, prickly berry bushes and sugar maples clinging to the granite of the Canadian Shield and surrounded by the untainted depths of a spring fed lake.

Grandpa's quit claim of three of the lake's six islands for $25 each in the 1920's had already provided three idyllic camping summers for our family, but the original transaction, now questioned, had come back to haunt Dad and Mom. Grandpa and Grandma had built a cottage on the island facing the farmhouse. Dad got first pick of the other two islands as he married someone who was willing to camp before a cottage could be built. As far as we kids were concerned there was no question in our hearts this portion of heaven legally and morally belonged to us.

Everyone agreed our island had the best swimming rock in the entire lake. I couldn't wait to jump in for the first swim of the summer. There were no indoor swimming pools in Weston at the time so we never swam during the winter. I hoped I could remember how. I had practiced so much the summer before that Mom and Dad announced that if my swimming was strong enough this summer it might, just might, be safe for us to stay on the island for the entire two month school holiday with Mom. Dad would only stay for his three-week holiday and aside from that commute on weekends. Mom insisted for that to happen she had to have something more substantial than a moldy tent.

In the first three weeks Dad and Grandpa hoped to construct a framed single room, twelve by sixteen feet, on top of cedar stringer foundation logs, fashioned from trees from our island. They'd tack screens across window openings along the front, facing the lake. He promised Mom he'd build shutters on later weekends, for protection against the rain.

Dad preferred living outdoors, or as close as possible to it, after being what he called "chained to a desk" all winter. "A few more weeks in the tent. By the end of my holidays we'll be living in the lap of luxury."

As we pushed off from shore I shifted in my seat in the bow, trying to look in all directions at once. "Don't rock the boat," Dad said over his shoulder between rowing strokes. Donna sat in the middle seat, Mom and Doug in the stern of our green rowboat that Grandpa had left on shore, ready for us. A few days earlier Dad had phoned the farm.

"Our ETA is mid-afternoon," he had called into the phone from Weston, using the Royal Air Force term for estimated time of arrival he had picked up when employed as a weather forecaster during the war. After receiving the news in the farmhouse kitchen Elwood sent Mary to row out to Grandpa's island with the message.

I let my hand drag in the water to test the temperature for swimming. Roger, our new mascot, stood nose into the breeze on the peak behind me as we began the half-mile trip to Loon Island.

Dad rowed us toward Grandma and Grandpa's island to thank them for leaving the boat for us. They'd been at the lake a few weeks already because Grandpa was retired from teaching. Side by side on their dock, I can still see them in my imagination, resplendent in red Hudson Bay wool shirts. Grandpa's covered his navy blue tartan shirt and gray paint spattered workpants. Grandma's hung long over her cotton housedress.

I half-listened to their conversation, impatiently swishing my fingers back and forth among the lily pads, eager to be home.

CHAPTER 8
COME FROM AWAY

May 15, 2015

"*H*ave you got the keys?" It's late afternoon as I dig into the outside pocket of my carry-on luggage and produce a heavily-laden key chain. We've been in the air five and a half hours: Kelowna, Calgary, Ottawa. About the same number of hours it took to drive from Weston to our family lake in the 50s.

"Yup. They're all together. Right here. House and car keys for SilverStar, car and cottage keys for here." The jangling mess weighs down my purse all winter. I don't mind. It's a heft that connects me to summer freedom, my heart-home and family. Barry leads the way out of the arrivals area, steers right.

"There it is. Right where Joe said it would be."

Joe's the owner of Canadian Classic vehicle storage where we store our little summer car for the winter alongside the fair-weather Rolls and Bentleys of the well-to-do in Ottawa. It's our second year of flying to the lake instead of driving across Canada. Barry rolls the luggage cart along the sidewalk of the VIP parking. He stops behind our humble but sporty stick shift charcoal gray Hyundai Elantra.

Our carbon fibre canoe paddles lie safely in the trunk where we left them last October. Last to leave the lake, we paddled to shore in Dad's old fibreglass canoe. We hid it in the bushes at the end of our family parking lot, the last field before the end of the road and the farmhouse now owned by cousin Mary and her husband Wayne Newport.

We never know for sure, now that we're all retired, who will *get to the lake first, so we leave a canoe to get to the island. We switch the paddles to the back seat to make room for our luggage and drive to the closest airport hotel. It's been a long day. Jet-lagged we head for a quick dinner and a sleepover.*

Relaxed and refreshed we set out the next morning for the two-hour drive to the lake. Barry has the schedule organized. "Let's stop at Westport for lunch, get groceries in Glenburnie and pick up your Nespresso coffee order at The Perth Road Convenience store." Sounds good to me. I love having a summer supply of coffee capsules waiting for me. That places us at the lake early afternoon, about the time I predicted as our ETA in my email to Doug.

Perth Road Village is our last stop before the turn off.

"When your coffee order arrived, I knew I'd see you soon. Welcome back," says the current postmaster at the Perth Road Convenience store on Hwy 10 just outside the village. I stow the coffee in the back seat with the groceries and paddles.

"Let's drive through the village so we'll know we've really arrived."

Barry turns off the highway, into history. Hughson's store is now someone's residence. All that remains of Scullion's is a few randomly scattered foundation blocks. The Catholic Church is a family home. The new Perth Road United Church stands beside the old, now a community hall used for Sunday School, the annual Giant Pie Sale and local Thanksgiving dinners.

We turn left off Hwy 10 onto the rough dirt lane. There's an official Department of Highways sign at the corner. It reads "Shales Road". My shoulders relax, I exhale slowly then lean forward for a look up at the canopy of maples closing over the road. I'm home.

I grab my cell phone and dial Doug's cottage number. I picture him answering. He's sitting in an easy chair, feet up on the ottoman, reading the Globe and Mail, waiting in front of Grandpa's fireplace, now his own.

"We're here," I say. "See you in a few minutes."

CHAPTER 9
A SUMMER OF FIRSTS

July 1951

Afgter our arrival at Loon Island that July day in 1951 we dutifully helped unload the boat. Then our first stop was the Front Rock. Once our bare feet touched the granite it was like we'd never been away.

Dad joined us. "The water level's a bit high for this time of year. If this sun keeps up, it'll go down soon."

Dad turned away from the lake, shoes squishing, toward higher ground.

"Doug, come and help with the tent. You girls give your Mom a hand."

Mom carried the boxes of groceries and cooking pots to the outdoor table.

"Put the milk and cheese in the icebox, Donna. It should be cold by now. Grandpa said he put ice in it for us this morning," Mom said.

No job assignments, I decided to show our new puppy, Roger, around the island. Always a bit nervous going into the woods alone, I felt bolder with Roger along. I passed the tall leafy sumac then ventured under the canopy of maple and oak. I kept my eyes open in case we met a prickly porcupine or sleek, playful otter. He raced ahead, often in circles, sniffing, wagging his fluffy puppy tail and peeing everywhere, marking his new territory. It was a struggle to keep up with him. In no time he had staked his claim. He rushed to investigate the scent of beaver at a chewed birch stump, then hesitated for an extra sniff in the shallows

Doug with Roger at the Front Rock. —Eileen Jamieson

along the shore, entranced by the odour of an otter slide. Muzzle close to the ground he found the aroma of opossum at the base of a tall eastern white cedar.

For him, a summer of firsts. His frantically wagging tail showed his obvious joy at being liberated from the rope attached at one end to his collar and the other to our suburban backyard clothesline. So many lessons to be learned. Pungent animal smells entertained him for hours. Too much tasty summer grass made him vomit. Soon, for him, as for us, life centred around our rugged chunk of granite, the front swimming rock.

Roger and I shared a lack of self-confidence before the first swim of the season. He raced to the water's edge, lapped up a few swallows, then turned away, not yet interested in the lake except as a huge drinking bowl. Donna and Doug dashed into the water. I followed, splashing behind them past the drop off. A moment of sheer terror triggered my muscle memory, automatically coaxing my arms and legs into furious action. Chin grazing the surface I turned and furiously dog-paddled my way back to shore.

Dark eyes clouded with worry, Roger sprinted back and forth along the granular stretch of rock. Beside himself, he barked and pranced, back and forth, never taking his eyes from us. His expression said rescue, but his body wouldn't cooperate. He had no idea how to go about it.

Like all of us, Roger began his swimming career playing in the shallows. With all three of us reassuring him, we coaxed him into the chilly early July water. The minnows and sunfish swirling around, tickling his feet, fascinated him. The shimmering schools of bluegill cavorting in the warmth created by the sun and rock mesmerized him. Tail up, chin grazing the surface he stared, hesitated, stock still, focused, then snapped, nose diving down into the water, in a vain attempt at catching a fish. He did, once. Once was enough. He dropped the shimmering morsel immediately, surprised by the uncomfortable mouthful of scales and raised fins.

The ice was usually gone from Draper Lake in early to mid-April. When the frozen sheets cracked and shifted in the spring, the force of the departing chunks often took a few docks with it. Ours, a slim catwalk banged together with leftover lumber, was no exception. Doug and Donna, the rowboat under the pathetic power of Uncle Orie's motor, cruised the lake to scan the shoreline and retrieve our dock.

From the first time Doug operated the outboard motor three years before, he looked at home in the stern of the small boat, hand on the throttle, in charge of the destination. Donna and I had our turns but that motor and the captain's position fell to him most often. On dock hunting excursions Doug and Donna often discovered docks belonging to Grandpa or Uncle Elwood's shoreline cottages. Old fishing docks, decrepit raft-like structures, lay jammed up against the shore of whatever bay the ice had dragged them into.

Roger's first summer there, Doug and Donna discovered the

perfect candidate for teaching Roger to swim. They tied the dilapidated raft to the rowboat and hauled it back to our island. For a few days we crossed our fingers. Neither Grandpa nor Dad could find out the owner. It was ours to keep.

The soggy platform barely floated, but like a cardboard box is to a toddler, that raft provided hours of entertainment for Doug and Donna. Roger and I were not always as amused. To begin Roger's swimming lessons, Donna and Doug edged the raft up to the Front Rock. At their invitation I edged my derriere over to the raft. Then all three of us cajoled Roger into joining us.

"C'mon. It's okay. We promise. It'll be fine."

Not a purebred, a mix of collie and German shepherd and reputedly the runt of the litter, he displayed an indecisive and timid demeanour. He repeatedly ventured one paw onto the raft, tested the stability, felt the platform slide away, then timidly stepped back. He and I shared a healthy trepidation. We both knew how it felt to be the youngest and the smallest. But unfailingly, time and time again, we succumbed to their trick. With Roger and me safely aboard, Doug and Donna, still in the water, flutter-kicked the waterlogged vessel past the ledge well out over the deep water. Roger sat beside me, trembling slightly. I draped a calming arm around his neck, our backs warmed by the afternoon sun. His gaze fixed longingly on the rapidly disappearing rock.

The soggy raft easily supported the weight of one small girl and one collie puppy. But then Donna and Doug crawled up onto opposite ends of the raft, so as to keep it balanced. "Ladies lingerie, going down."

The raft slowly sank, leaving just their heads above water, under our collective weight. Every time they found it hilarious and slightly risqué to call out this phrase, which they claimed to have heard from an elevator operator at the T. Eaton Company in downtown Toronto. Shorter-legged creatures like Roger and me were left to our own devices as the raft sank below us under Doug and Donna's weight. I dog-paddled for shore. Roger swam in circles, his anxious expression darting from one of us to the other. He couldn't decide which of us he should be saving or which of us he could scramble up onto to save himself. We swam close enough to encourage him toward shore but distant enough to prevent getting scratched by his desperately scrambling claws.

All summer he wore out the rock and his paws with constant back and forth traffic, dunking for fish and swimming back from the raft. Exhausted, he collapsed on the warm rock, licked at and whimpered over the blistered pads of his tender suburban soles. His feet got tougher over the summer. So did ours.

Each evening, following the usual visits to the spitting rock and the split log, the same issue arose. We gathered as usual on the tent floor ready to hold our breath for the bolt through the lingering haze of DDT.

"Please can we let Rodger Codger in tonight?" The three of us affected our most soulful expressions. "He always looks so lonely out here." We tried every night. Usually the answer was no. "His coat is full of mosquitoes." Most nights he curled up outside the tent door, his rump indenting the canvas in our direction.

One evening, when sinister clouds threatened a thunderstorm, Mom and Dad relented. "Give his coat a good brushing with your hands." That done we lined up, ready to dash in. "Okay, one, two, three, go!" Dad opened the flaps to a slit just wide enough for us to enter. We snuggled under the covers. Roger circled at our feet, then settled. We fell asleep to the sound of buzzing mosquitoes. After that he was left outside and forced to content himself with one last good night snuggle. Still, he nuzzled his tawny and white snout between the flaps and into the tent. We patted him on the nose, then tightened the ties. Resigned to his fate, he followed his tail around in circles on the rough boards outside the tent opening and finally plopped down with a sigh of dejected disgust.

Dad and Grandpa toiled away every day of Dad's holiday on the construction of a rustic four by eight metre screened cottage for us. Dad's correspondence with the Department of Lands and Forests had finally resulted in an ultimatum. The latest letter received the month before stipulated that Dad and Mom had to pay for the island and build a cottage within two years. If they didn't they would forfeit ownership. Dad surrendered to the inevitable. The Department of Lands and Forests had decided against honouring the quit claim deed.

Dad wrote back and agreed to pay. Then, another, even more threatening challenge: their response began several more years of increasingly heated missives of how and during what time of year the island should be measured and what price could be agreed on.

"That'll keep them for a few months." Pushing away from his desk in the master bedroom of our suburban home, Dad's last act before leaving the city for his holidays had been composition of yet another letter stating his argument for what he considered a fair price. We couldn't believe the island still wasn't legally ours.

Dad and Grandpa start by sweeping a relatively flat portion of higher ground, a platform of Canadian Shield granite about six metres back from the lake. The threat of having to buy back the land from the Canadian government at an exorbitant price, or perhaps leftover attitudes of the Great Depression and World War II, led Dad to scrimp on materials. He and Grandpa bushwhacked around the island. They choose four tall, straight cedars from the high spot in the middle of the island. They felled the fifty-foot cedars with a crosscut saw, working together, one on either side of the tree. After trimming the larger branches, they dragged the logs through the bush back to the building site. On site they trimmed the remaining branches and knots. Thrilled to be involved, Doug helped by stripping the bark with his hatchet. Axe in motion, Dad crudely flattened the logs along one side. Side by side, three generations hauled and prepared to place the logs as stringers for the floor joists. Mom supervised, arms folded across the plaid of one of Dad's old shirts. As construction foreman she stepped over one of the foundation logs then glanced back over her shoulder toward the lake to scrutinize the view.

"A little to the left," Mom said. Dad bent over, shifted the log, eyeballed the angle and glanced up at Mom, one eyebrow raised.

"That's good. Now it's parallel to the shoreline. It'll be a great view of the sunrise."

"Are you sure, Anne?"

He turned to Doug and Grandpa. " Okay. Set her down." By the end of Dad's holiday the basic shell of the cottage was complete.

While mathematically sound, the resulting structure didn't measure up to code. In 1950 the space required between upright building studs sat at a maximum of 24 inches, known as two-foot centres. Dad placed his studs 36 inches apart to save lumber costs, creating three-foot centres. To his credit he used hardy spruce studs, full-sized two by fours, not the scaled down version available today. Thin rows of cove siding, nailed tightly one above the other, formed outside walls. The front wall facing the lake opened waist high. Dad stretched rolled screening from one end of the building to the other, then nailed it in place at window level, allowing a stellar view of the lake. Sweat dripping off his back from the afternoon sun, he covered the roof, also built on three-foot centers, with inexpensive rolled roofing and spread copious gobs of black tar sealant along the overlapping seams.

"I promise to start building the window shutters next time we're back. The leftover siding cuts will work well for that. I'll hang them outside the screens," Dad said.

Mom was not convinced. "They'll make the cottage awfully dark, especially on rainy days." She hoped it wouldn't be too long before they could afford windows.

"I'll take a look at the wreckers in Kingston next time we're in town. They might have something that'll fit," Dad said.

You could tell by Mom's wrinkled forehead that she wasn't holding out hope. Our family rarely ventured away from the lake.

In the meantime, for dull rainy days and after dark, Dad fastened two red tin coal oil lamps high on one interior wall, well out of the way of us rambunctious kids. One wrong move with a lit flame could spell disaster.

Mom surveyed the interior, her private blank canvas. "I'm going to need some shelving."

Under Mom's watchful eyes Dad built several wide, high shelves along the back wall to organize the area that would serve as her kitchen. He attached two recently acquired kerosene burners, each large enough to support her campfire-blackened cooking pots, to the top boards. In the lower shelf Mom stacked mugs and dishes. Two orange crates below housed cans and boxes of food as well as the waterproof tin of wooden matches. Kerosene came in a large pail with a pouring spout. Dad stored it outside behind the cottage.

"Where do you want the icebox?" Arms crossed, Mom surveyed her domain.

"How about in the corner, at the end of the shelves. Two camp chairs and our kids' mattress completed the interior décor.

One evening about twenty years later Donna and I were doing dishes in the kitchen addition, now equipped with electricity and running water. The large family gathering had necessitated using all the extra dishes, including some of the old dishes left over from our camping days. Washing and drying our indestructible Melmac bowls brought back loads of memories. The red tin coal oil lamps still hung safely on the wall on either side of a new fireplace. Lost in thought I dried my personal silver spoon, the one with the teddy bear on the handle.

"We were really lucky to get to sleep inside. Wonder why Mom and Dad always preferred the tent."

Donna, by then the mother of four daughters gave me a sideways glance. "What don't you get?"

Already married once, and divorced, I was no innocent. But surprisingly it had never before dawned on me why Mom and Dad preferred to sleep in the tent until Dad finally got around to building a private master bedroom.

"So that's why they let us sleep in the cottage alone. I thought they were training us to be brave." Laughing, I grabbed my pink Melmac plate from the drying rack. "How stupid could we be?"

I placed the plate on the shelf with Donna's blue one and Doug's green one. "And, I thought they were just being martyrs, leaving us all the space in the cottage. Now I know why Dad always sang that old camp song "Tenting Tonight" with such a smile."

Even then, Mom and Dad acted like they were on their honeymoon.

Dad's three-week holiday went by in a flash of crimson sunrises, orange campfires and flaming sunsets. A few days before we were scheduled to return to the city, Mom and Dad sat us down on the bench by our outdoor table.

"Your mother and I have a surprise for you. How would you like to stay in the new cottage with Mom during the week? I'll come back next weekend. We'll see how one week goes."

We couldn't believe our ears. Now all three of us could swim well enough, it would be safe to stay with Mom alone. No long, hot drive back to the city. No boring nights in suburbia. Living in the woods without Dad would be a huge step for Mom, the Beach Girl.

"Grandpa will come over to check on you every day to see if you need anything," Dad looked at us, but his statement was probably more for Mom's benefit than ours.

"If it works, can we stay all summer?" Doug's eyes widened, owl-sized. Donna and I held our breath, waiting for the response.

"That's up to your mother. We'll see how it goes." We learned early on that they discussed family issues privately, then presented us with a united front.

Sunday after dinner Donna, Roger and I joined Mom on the dock. Dad hugged us and kissed Mom.

"Listen to your mother." He sounded more serious than usual.

"No swimming without an adult."

We watched him row away, his broad shoulders diminishing, smaller and smaller. For the first time he'd drive back to Toronto alone. Doug sat grinning in the stern, proud of his responsibility to row back alone. The reliable rowboat stayed at our dock as it served as our only means of transportation from the island.

Next Friday evening Grandpa would tow it to the shore. We'd be waiting to hear the honk of Dad's car horn, signalling his return. We knew we'd miss him but were delirious with our good fortune. We could stay on our island.

We were ecstatic about our palatial screened cottage.

"Call it a porch," dad said. Thinking ahead, he already hoped the building would satisfy the boys at Lands and Forests while not creating a high tax bill once we officially owned the land.

"It was never meant to be the Taj Mahal." Dad grinned. "I built it as a shelter to get out of the rain."

Despite the simplicity of the building, he stood a little bit taller, proud of providing a cottage to make his Beach Girl more comfortable.

We had an island cottage, but, as yet, no idea how much it would cost to keep it.

Many years passed before I fully understood the extent of the sacrifices Mom and Dad made to keep the island. Our practical, stay-at-home Mom pinched pennies, clipped grocery coupons for the A & P (The Great Atlantic and Pacific Tea Company), canned peaches, pears and cherries, made do with home permanents, and sewed sundresses for herself, for Donna and for me. Dad clocked up extra independent hours for other insurance companies. He set up a carpool. Canada Life colleagues willingly paid for the comfortable one-hour commute in our family car from their doorstep in the suburbs to the downtown Toronto office. Our parents never worried us with talk of the second mortgage on our house in Weston, the only way they could afford to buy the island. They never complained or discussed money issues in front of us. There was never any question: the island was ours and would remain in the Shales family.

CHAPTER 10
HGTV RENO PLANS

July 2017

"*A*re you up for a stroll over to the Front Rock?" Barry looks up from his iPad. He closes the program, a whitewater canoeing instructional video, then stands and stretches. *A red sunset flames across the water on our side of the island. There was a time I considered this spot as a long distance away from our original cottage site and our Front Rock. Before we retired Barry acted as construction foreman with Doug, Donna's husband Art and me as his workers, to build our bunkie for us on the back of the island.*

Five minutes later we're sitting on the Front Rock watching the long shimmering reflection of the moon executing a slow dive into the lake, as it simultaneously rises over the point past Doug and Margo's cottage. It's been almost thirty years since they inherited Grandpa and Grandma's island.

Our original cottage, the ' "Main Lodge" ' as we now facetiously call it, still stands behind us, barely. Since our parents passing and Donna's death in 2015, Doug and I own the island and cottage. The bedrooms Dad built on the end of the cottage sink slowly into the lowland at that end of the building. The kitchen and the bathroom on the back are shifting, a little more with each season. Only the master bedroom, constructed on solid granite, stands firm. The front lawn remains the most popular gathering place for family. Our nieces and nephews, Doug and Donna's grandchildren and our special family friends still enjoy the cottage for overnight visits.

"Doug wants to tear down the back bedrooms. They're twisting away from the living room." *I have to agree. It makes me sad to see our former haven in such a neglected condition.*

"He's right. It's not safe the way it is. We shouldn't really let anyone stay in it the way it is," Barry says as he looks over his shoulder. Moonlight illuminates the windows Dad finally put in to replace the screens. The collection of shutters leans against the side wall, waiting to be hung in the fall to protect the windows from winter storms.

"Dad let me help paint the shutters. Must have been only six or seven. We worked outside so I guess it didn't matter if I made a mess. I learned so many skills here," I say.

I wonder how long the demolition will take. Doug hopes once the back bedrooms are gone the main room will be more stable.

"If Doug wants to keep the kitchen and bathroom, he's going to have to jack them up some more." I can almost see Barry's brain considering the problem. The slant of the kitchen floor makes me nervous, too. The old electric Frigidaire weighs heavily at one end of the small addition.

"And I never thought it would come to this but I guess we should paint the interior walls, at least the back wall. It's so black from the years of cooking on kerosene burners. Maybe if we paint the exterior grey I can do that wall a pale gray to make the room lighter," I say, remembering the light hue of the original wood when the walls were first built.

We stroll back along the path to our side of the island. "I'll call Doug in the morning. We can get started when all the kids have gone back to school in September. Senior siblings cottage reno starts in September. It'll be just like HGTV," I say.

CHAPTER 11
TEA, A BIG FISH AND A TALL SILK HAT

August 1952

The shrill whistle of the kettle boiling for tea on the kerosene burner blasted from inside the cottage. Mom was ready to entertain.

Mom stood erect, shoulders relaxed, in front of the new side screen door. Dad had just put the last brush strokes of paint on the newly completed building. Hands in her pockets, the Beach Girl's posture radiated confidence. Flared shorts accentuated her slim waist, topped with a high-necked halter. Cut in at the shoulders, the pale cotton showed off her athletic arms, tanned from the necessities and joys of island cottage life. Rowing, swimming and constantly sweeping bits of cedar and dark soil brought in by three sets of bare feet, Mom operated at whirlwind speed. Forever plagued by low arches and flat feet, she wore sensible lace up shoes. Donna, now ten, already a self-appointed member of the pre-teen fashion police, considered Mom almost as unfashionable as Aunt Hazel.

Growing up a preacher's kid, Mom helped her mom, Annie Melinda Mae, my Grandma Gordon, host parishioners at social events at home in the manse and in various church halls. In those days ministers in the United Church accepted an assignment in different churches every four years. By necessity, Mom and her siblings, my Uncle Doug and Auntie Allison, changed schools with each move. They learned early how to make the best of the situation, how to make new school friends. Their summer cottage at Bruce Beach served as a secure, solid home base. Mom shone at social gatherings, in her element smashing balls around in tennis tournaments at Bruce Beach or sashaying across boards of the sprung dance floor at the Kincardine Pavillion.

Dad, a self-described introvert, appreciated Mom's easy manner with extended family and friends.

"Your mother has the talent to make the simplest get-together into a special event where everyone feels welcome."

All summer at Draper Lake she did just that.

Once Dad completed the original room of the cottage, he felt ready to begin his next ambitious project, which would last for several summers. For a few hours each day of his holidays and summer weekends he could be found digging clay marl out of the area where we docked our boats. He'd put his coffee cup down after breakfast, smile at Mom and head out to grab his shovel.

"I think I'll do a bit of dredging before it gets too hot." He methodically shoveled marl from under the surface of the water into a wheelbarrow he borrowed from Uncle Elwood, then rolled the sludgey bounty through the shallow water and emptied it into the lowest area of the swamp. Load by load he raised the level of the ground, filling in the swamp. This painstakingly slow method of landscaping kept him wet up to the bottom hem of his swimming trunks all day. He stayed cool and enjoyed the physical exertion never afforded at his desk job.

His vision of the future sustained his efforts, summer after summer, as he set the stage for generations of family traditions. He imagined extended family and friends competing in raucous games of croquet, badminton and volleyball on an expansive lawn. No more swampy, scary route to the Front Rock. Perhaps he envisioned Mom leading singsongs surrounded by smiling faces, radiant in the glow of an evening campfire. Maybe he even predicted the scene of large family events: Mom, the matriarch, presiding over afternoon tea, lineups of cousins waiting for turns to jump off the diving board he would build, Roger frantically running back and forth along the Front Rock, while parents lifeguarded from the comfort of lawn chairs.

He alternated layers of muck and hayseed swept from the floor of Uncle Elwood's barn to fill in the swamp. In later years, when he could afford it, he topped the mixture with grass seed. Thanks to Dad's dream and perseverance we ended up with not only the best place to swim on the lake but the go-to spot for aquatic and field sports as well as social activities for family and friends.

Along the border of the deeper docking area Dad assembled a wall with the rocks he found in the muck.

Mom loved it. "It's just like the shoreline walls on the Big Rideau Lake. Now all we need is a couple of willow trees."

"Maybe no willow trees. I prefer to keep things 'au naturel'," he said, with a wink in Mom's direction.

Two long springy catwalks, 60 cm wide boards nailed onto cedar stringers, reached out from the shore. One acted as a docking spot for our rowboat and Miss Niagara. The other remained open for guests.

Donna, Mom and me at the front swimming rock early 50's. —Eileen Jamieson

The most vivid tea party I remember wasn't about tea at all. What happened after the tea was poured and sipped sticks in my brain. As usual, precisely at 3 p.m., when the kettle whistled, the usual suspects, Dad's brother Dave and his family, pulled into the guest dock. As dictated by what our family considered proper island etiquette, Doug grabbed the bow rope to help guide their boat alongside the dock. By this time Uncle Dave and Aunt Gladys had started construction of a cottage on their own island, also a wedding gift to them. Dad feared his brother's request for a formal building permit and plans for a grand cottage built by hired professionals would alert the department of Lands and Forests to the existence of our tiny screened in cottage. Dad kept silent on the issue, never allowing the matter to cause a rift in family solidarity.

Dad extended a hand to assist his sister-in-law, Aunt Gladys, to step up onto the dock. Dad described his older brother as a "big business man", with the emphasis on big. Like Dad, Uncle Dave was chained to a desk as Vice-President at CIL Paint in Montreal, but he hadn't remained as active as Dad.

Only when Dad and Aunt Gladys reached solid ground did he step out of his boat, carrying two camp chairs. His sons followed: our cousin Kenny, aged six like me, and his brother David Junior, the same age as Donna. We kids headed for the swimming rock and the adults settled next to Grandma and Grandpa who had arrived earlier.

As kids we considered Grandma's oatmeal cookies the only interesting thing about afternoon tea. After eating as many as allowed, usually two each to start, we soon bored of listening to the adults talking. We swam for a while, then the older kids went off exploring the island searching for a good place to build a fort. Kenny and I dug holes in the shell beach area, filled cans, overturned them and created a village. When that got boring, I wandered over to the adult circle.

"Dad, can I go fishing?"

"Sure, but you probably won't catch much in the middle of the afternoon."

Given the go ahead I retrieved my pole from behind the cottage then braved the edge of the remaining swampy area to go frog hunting. The area where the grass remained long teemed with frogs. I easily spotted the nose of an unsuspecting green leopard frog partially camouflaged by reeds. Silently I crouched down and with one practiced swoosh of my right hand it was mine. My empathy for frogs had not yet blossomed. I grabbed my bamboo pole and firmly held the small creature in my left hand. Then I ruthlessly jabbed the metal hook into its throat. The barb protruded out the back of its head, exactly the way Dad had taught us. With no consideration for the feelings of the frog, I headed for the Front Rock to try my luck.

It turns out standing thigh deep in warm lake water in middle of a sunny afternoon wasn't a wise idea. I thought I had found the perfect place for fishing. I stood in the shallow water, without a sun hat, becoming drowsier by the minute. It seemed like hours. Probably only ten minutes had gone by without a nibble on what I deemed a delicious looking frog. And so, I started to play with my ten-foot bamboo pole. My arm muscles quickly cramped and tired holding the long pole in the right position so that the line stayed clear of the drop off.

I had insisted on being allowed to fish. I couldn't just give up. Instead, I let the pole float on the water. It worked. The end of the pole was far enough out and the line remained clear of the rock. However, my big mistake was when I took my hands off the pole. At that precise moment a hefty bass decided to swallow the little green frog, and the hook.

In a flash the pole jerked away toward the black water, then disappeared, reappearing in an upright position about ten feet away well out in the deep water. Two feet of the pole stood vertically above the surface. The other eight feet had submerged with the fish.

I stared in disbelief. The pole twitched and trembled frantically, as if possessed. Would I get the heck for losing my pole? Finally I took a big breath and yelled.

"Dad. My pole." With that the drowsy sunny afternoon reverted to chaos.

Dad and my Uncle Dave bolted out of their armchairs and ran for a boat. Roger barked. My arm stretched out in a helpless point as I stood gawking at the bamboo pole. Family members leapt out of chairs, gazes fixed toward the commotion beyond the swimming rock. Dad and Uncle Dave rowed out. Dave steadied the boat while Dad grabbed the end of the pole and wrangled the feisty culprit into the boat.

"I guess some fish do like to bite in the afternoon," Grandpa said.

I met them back at the dock. Dad held up the shimmering beauty. The end of one tiny frog leg protruded from its jaw. As usual, Grandpa, our family photographer, had his camera close at hand.

"What a whopper," Dad said. "We have to get a picture." He passed the heavy fish closer. I stepped back. "Put your hand through the gills the way I showed you before."

I had never encountered a fish this large up close and personal.

"No way. It's too big and the teeth are too sharp." I stepped further away.

We struck a compromise. Dad found a sturdy stick. He shoved it through the gills of the gasping bass. I agreed to hold one end of the stick. "Stand up straight, and smile."

I did try, but my arms trembled with the weight of the fish. Grandpa looked down into his camera. I puffed up my skinny chest, lungs swelled with the self-importance of a seasoned fisherman.

"Got it," said Grandpa. Donna looked on in admiration.

"Lucky catch," Doug said, his tone revealing a bit of jealousy.

Before dinner Dad gave me my first and only lesson in cleaning fish. We threw the guts into the lake. "That'll be a treat for the turtles," said Dad as he threw the guts out into the shallow water in front of First Rock.

For Christmas that year Doug bought me a Santa Claus piggy bank with his paper route money. I slipped every coin from my allowance and the occasional bill from special occasion gifts through the slot on the top of Santa's head. The next summer I purchased my own pale green fibreglass fishing rod with a reel.

Later that summer Dad built a partition up to the top level of the wall studs near one end of the cottage to divide off a bedroom to allow privacy for an overnight guest. Mom sewed and hung a curtain across the doorway. Mom and Dad still preferred to sleep in the tent. Behind the divider, inside the partitioned off area, three cots lay side-by-side with three wooden-slatted orange crates to house our growing collection of Superman, Lulu, Archie, Mickey Mouse and Classic comic books. Taking care not to rustle the pages we read under the covers well past our assigned bedtime illuminated by our Disney character flashlights. Mine was shaped like Mickey

Patti and her big fish. —Will Shales

Mouse's dog Pluto. When I pushed the tail, his nose lit up. Unfortunately, if I pointed it in the wrong direction, the red glow of the blanket alerted Mom and Dad, cutting reading time short for that night.

Mom and Dad invited Eileen Jamieson, our wintertime babysitter, as our first and all time favourite overnight guest. Jamie, as everyone called her, lived a few blocks away from us in Weston. Her long wavy raven hair, generous smile and young, single working girl status gave her an air of independence and glamour. In her mid-twenties she was a few years younger and several inches taller than Mom. Jamie longed to start a family but her long-time boyfriend was dragging his feet.

Anticipation and excitement culminated when we heard the blast of Dad's car horn on the Friday evening. We were thrilled about Jamie's arrival with Dad.

"That's it. One long, one short," said Mom while clearing the dinner dishes. Doug jumped in the rowboat. The motor started on the first pull. He sped to shore to pick them up. Mom, Donna and I waited at the dock. Every year Jamie spent her annual two-week holiday with us, an escape from her clerical office position with a Weston contractor. She reveled in the cottage experience. Mom enjoyed adult company and someone to share the responsibility for us during the week. We got time with one of our favourite people outside our nuclear family. Even Roger loved Jamie. Until his death at the age of seventeen Jamie remained the only human Roger trusted other than family members.

Mom was proud to show Jamie our cottage.

"I'll put your bag down behind the partition. There's a mattress for you beside the kids. When Doug goes back to work you can join me in the tent."

Jamie had never been to an island cottage and had never slept in a tent. Mom's smile radiated at the notion of adult company when Dad was gone. We couldn't wait to show the island to our favourite person outside our nuclear family.

Despite continued twilight doses of DDT to the screen door, Roger was banished most nights to sleep in the shallow space created by the foundation logs under the cottage. Sometimes, when Jamie slept in the tent with Mom, we snuck him in with us. Occasionally Mom relented, most often when we heard him whining during a thunderstorm, traumatized by chaotic booms of thunder and zig zag flashes of chain lightning so common in Ontario thunderstorms. Only then Mom gave us the nod. We'd rush out in the rain to discover him crouched low, cold and damp, under the cottage. Tail wagging furiously he'd follow us inside where we'd rub him down with an old towel then settle contentedly on the floor between our cots.

Jamie exhibited legendary patience. On rainy days she joined us at Grandpa's rickety card table through never ending rounds of Crokinole, Monopoly, Canasta and Double Solitaire in the dim lamplight of the shuttered cottage. When the rain stopped, we burst outside to sit lined up on the rock watching Mom and Jamie have their turn to swim first. Jamie's effortless front crawl matched Mom's smooth execution. Later, towels spread on the rough granite, for comfort as well as the preservation of their bathing suits, the two friends sat side-by-side, chatting, lifeguarding, shelling peas and peeling potatoes.

Shortly before dark one evening Jamie supervised Doug and Donna sharpening the ends of swamp maple branches in preparation for a special campfire. For days we'd begged, pleaded and finally persuaded Mom and Jamie to undertake what, to us, seemed a grand adventure. They loaded several picnic baskets, folding chairs and a couple of flashlights into the rowboat. Mom rowed, Roger and I took our usual spot in the peak, Donna, Doug and Jamie wedged in across the stern seat. We glided our way about a half-mile across the silky stillness of dusk to the far shore. Mom steered the rowboat into a cove and grounded gently into the shallows.

She stepped gingerly onto the slanted granite rock of this mysterious shoreline delineating the edge of an abandoned lead mine at the back of a local farm. We waited. She stood still a moment. Peered into the forest.

"Looking for bears?" Donna's whisper accompanied her mischievous grin.

"Shhh. No, humans." It was, after all, private property. But, as the farmer rarely appeared on the shore, we considered it an extension of our private playground. Our status as the only kids from an island gave us an entitled sense of belonging. We were in love with our lake, our island and its surroundings. This terrain, this water, gave us our identity.

In a small clearing in the forest Mom and Jamie set up a campfire in a circle with rocks we'd carried from the shore. When the flames died down to produce glowing coals, Jamie produced squares of homemade rolled pastry dough from under a tea towel in one of the baskets.

"Bring your sticks over." Jamie showed us how to wrap the dough around. "Turn the stick slowly just above the coals. Keep turning until the dough turns light brown." We rotated our sticks until we could no longer stand the heat and hunger.

"Mine's done," I said, taking it over to Jamie. She helped each of us slide the dough off the end of the stick. Mom dribbled spoonfuls of Aunt Alice's raspberry jam into the opening. Partially raw, painstakingly charred to a glorious blistering temperature, dripping with hot red juices. We devoured the pastries with sighs of delight.

To round out the night Jamie taught us a new campfire song, "My Tall Silk Hat". Sung to the traditional melody of "Finculi, Finicula," Jamie taught us the parody of the original penned in 1933 by Arthur Fields and Fred Hall. The lyrics seemed impossibly exotic. We found the story of the gentleman's hat being sat upon by ' "a big fat lady" ' absolutely hilarious.

"Let's sing it again," we chanted over and over.

Jamie holds up the days catch. —Will Shales

Somewhere there's a photo of that campfire. Did Doug have his own Brownie camera by that time or was it Jamie's? Somehow the small square flashbulb attachment worked. The photo shows two women wearing casual collared shirts over wrinkled shorts, hair comfortably messed, lounging on folding camp chairs. Beside them, two young girls and a dog lean forward over the embers, toward the waning warmth, no doubt trying to avoid the mosquitoes. Jamie's face glows with inner kindness. The light of the campfire creates a circle of care and love, a safe haven from the darkness of the surrounding forest.

On the return trip Jamie switched seats with Mom, rowing us home under the stars, our voices echoing across the stillness. Mom's clear contralto, honed from years in church choirs, led us in "Stars are The Windows of Heaven" a haunting song by Jimmy Steiger and Tommy Malie, first made popular by The Andrews Sisters in 1950.

Mom started us off.

"Two little kids watching the skies
One of them says I wonder why
All of the stars are shining so bright
When there wasn't a star last night?"

We joined in, Donna already adept at finding the alto line to harmonize with Mom's commanding contralto.

We gazed skyward as we sang the final lines.

"My mom says stars are the windows of heaven
Where angels peep through."

CHAPTER 12
JAMIE'S MAPLE

Saturday, August 4, 2012

*T*he screen door slams behind me as I step out onto the front deck of our cottage. "I'm heading over to the Front Rock. It's almost time for tea." Barry looks up from his latest project. He's building an extension on the deck to house our new barbecue.

"I'll be over in a while. Just have a few more boards to install."

"OK. See you in a bit." Then I remember our niece Kerry's kids have asked to try our kayaks. I look back up and call out, "Why don't you paddle the whitewater kayak over. The kids want to learn wet exits."

I place a quick peck on the clear spot on his cheek above his white beard. I grab my sunhat, towel, goggles and a container of chocolate chip cookies fresh out of the oven. I'm already dressed for swimming. I follow the path from our side of the island. Minutes later I'm surrounded by three generations of family. There's a badminton game in progress on the lawn, a gaggle of pre-teen boys and girls lined up along the Front Rock for turns at waterskiing and wakeboarding. Off to the side a curly-haired blond girl digs her plastic shovel into the marl beach.

At precisely three o'clock brother Doug steers his daughter Kerry's navy and white fibreglass inboard motor speedboat alongside the sturdy diving board raft he has attached at one end of the Front Rock.

"That's all the turns for now. No more until I've had my tea."

One of the kids ties the boat. Doug strides across the lawn through the impromptu badminton game. He collapses on a chair in the shade next to a round table strewn with thermoses, containers of hummus, crackers and cut veggies. I place my cookie contribution *in the melee. We hear the kettle whistle from inside the old family cottage, The Main Lodge. Donna, now sixty-six, emerges with a tray of cups, cream and sugar and a fresh pot of tea in Mom's blue and white pot.*

The circle of ten plastic and wooden Muskoka chairs accommodates only half the crowd. "Milk in first?" Donna serves the adults. She's joined us from her cottage around the corner. Children follow Doug from the Front Rock. Kerry pours milky tea from the thermos into plastic mugs. She serves all the kids, her own four and their cousins. "No cookies until you've had a few veggies." Kerry arrived last week with four kids, and her babysitter Holli, from her home in Los Angeles. They'll spend five weeks at the lake, based out of the shoreline log house Kerry and her husband Barry had built a decade ago. In true Ontario cottage tradition, Kerry's Barry will join the family for two weeks. A couple of statuesque LA blonds, Kerry and Holli make a great team, reminiscent of Mom and Jamie. The kids and cousins adore Holli. We all consider her a member of the family.

"Any cookies left?" My Barry calls out from the whitewater kayak as he approaches the Front Rock. "Who wants to learn a wet exit?"

Some actors, greying and wrinkled, show their age. Some, lithe and energetic, enter the scene for the first time. So many activities and traditions have stood the test of time. New ones have been welcomed. The stage remains, the grass and granite theatre, still housing a platform for the next acts of family events.

Late June 2021

"Notice anything new?" Doug says.

He and I pause beside the spitting rock, on the spot where the tent floor used to be. We are on an early season tour of the island. Early season for me, that is. We arrived the day before, the island a welcome ending to our leisurely road trip from SilverStar mountain in Vernon, British Columbia. Covid conditions forced us to stay home the summer of 2020. Not yet ready to board an airplane, and a second missed summer out of the question, we decided to drive.

Doug's been at the lake, off and on, since April. The three-hour drive from his home in Oakville, Ontario isn't enough to deter him from coming down to check our various family cottage properties the minute the ice is out of the lake.

"What am I supposed to be seeing?" My gaze follows the swivel of my body.

"Getting warmer," says Doug, giving me a clue we used in childhood games of I Spy. I look up the hill behind the cottage where the outhouse used to be. My eyes stop to admire a stately maple. That's when I notice the new carved wooden sign at the base of the trunk. It reads, "Jamie's Maple".

"Do you know how it got that name?" Still a big brother, Doug loves to quiz me about family lore.

"You think you know everything. Just like when we were kids." Secretly I'm glad I know this one. "Yes, I do. It's because Dad wanted to cut it to make a straight path to the outhouse.

"It's only small. Who cares?" I remember Dad had said.

But Jamie loved that maple. She persuaded him to put the path around it instead of cutting it down.

"We almost lost in in the Bastille Day storm in '95. Do you remember what happened?" Doug says.

"Yup. By then Dad had grown attached to it, so he took care of it for Jamie," I say.

Jamie had died of cancer some ten years before. The morning after the storm Dad found the tree half uprooted by the hurricane force winds and clinging to the side of the hill. He looped a rope around the trunk as high as he could reach and pulled the tree upright. Determined, he drove a wooden stake further up the hill and tied the tree to it.

"He left that rope on the tree for about five years," Doug says.

Doug removed the rope after Dad died.

"Now it's happy on its own. How could I forget that story, or Jamie?" I say.

CHAPTER 13
INDEPENDENCE

1953

The summer I turned seven Grandma chose a calm, sunny afternoon to volunteer as my personal rowing instructor. We'd been baking her signature oatmeal cookies all afternoon in her tiny cottage kitchen. Now it was almost time for tea, time for me to go back to our island and present Mom with some freshly baked treats.

"Would you like to row?" Grandma had never asked me that before. In the kitchen she stood with elegant posture, measured ingredients precisely and rarely smiled. Once the screen door of her cottage slammed behind her, her demeanor softened. She settled in the stern seat and smoothed the hem of her cotton housedress dress around her knees. I sat in the rower's position. Not a ripple disturbed the dark emerald surface of the lake. The oars looked long and heavy to me. I never knew if Grandpa purchased them or crafted them himself. The length was fine for Grandpa's boat. That day I discovered Grandma's oars were the same length. But Grandma's boat was narrower than Grandpa's. As a result, the oars overlapped at the grips. I had to take special care not to bash my knuckles.

My fingers didn't quite reach around the handles. My arm muscles tensed under their considerable weight.

"Keep your right hand a bit higher than your left. That way you won't bang your thumbs."

Exercising incredible patience, Grandma coached me as I did my best to heave the blades of the oars in even, matching strokes.

Grandma's gray rowboat 2021. —Patti Shales Lefkos

When the blades sliced the water gently below the surface, the boat moved ahead. When I forgot to keep my right hand higher, I crushed the knuckles of my left hand with the right oar and the boat stood still. My thumbs took a beating. Somehow I persevered. Maybe it was in my DNA to persevere, resilience passed down from generations of Shales battling to farm and feed their families here.

"That's good. Pull a bit harder on your left." Too hard. The boat spun in a circle.

"Now on your right. Not quite so hard." The bow spun back facing in the general direction of our dock.

It seemed to take forever before I could row from their island to ours in some semblance of a straight line, especially if there was any wind. Inherited stubbornness reinforcing my bones, I never considered giving up. With Grandma's guidance my aching arms learned to turn, maneuver the boat in reverse and smoothly edge it in next to any dock. My skill and confidence grew with every stroke.

Charlie Green, who lived in Perth Road Village, built Grandpa's boat. Soon after, Grandma had put her foot down.

"You can't leave me here without a boat when you go fishing," Grandma said. A strong Victorian woman, Grandma knew how to speak her mind, a trait I admired.

So Grandpa set up shop in Uncle Elwood's long, low drive shed, the storage area for the buggy, sled and team of Clydesdales. Elwood turned the horses out into the field to free up the space for boat building. With the assistance of a local carpenter he built a smaller version of his own boat, while my brother Doug watched, a preschooler at the time.

"I remember Aunt Alice carrying pots of water boiled on the woodstove. The men laid the planks on a bed of woodchips, then poured the water along the length of them. The heat of the water steamed the heavy planks, enough to bend them for the sides," Doug said.

Grandpa painted both boats battleship gray with maroon trim to match their cottage. Sturdily built rowboats, now painted red, these timeless vessels still provide reliable transport to and from the islands, seven decades later. With every pull against the wind I unknowingly channeled the strength willed to me by my robust ancestors.

During childhood I never wondered about our family's social or financial status. Kids at our school seemed the same. Members of the congregation of our local United Church were just like us: white, middle class, suburban post-war families. We went home to bungalows or modest two-storey brick homes in quiet neighbourhoods lined with grassy boulevards redolent with newly planted maple trees. Dads went to work. Moms stayed home with the kids.

Despite our obvious life of privilege, it was obvious we weren't wealthy.

"I'm sick of Donna's hand-me-downs. She always gets the new stuff." My jealousy flared when Donna got something new for school every fall.

"Doug's got a paper route. Donna does chores for her allowance. When you're old enough to earn money, you can buy your own new clothes," Mom countered.

We didn't eat out in restaurants. Weekends and after school we had scads of unscheduled time on our hands, mostly spent playing baseball at Merrill Municipal Park at the end of our street. When snow engulfed the neighbourhood we played road hockey. Our family owned the goalie nets we set up on the street in front of our house. We scuffled through snow drifts and took shots well past dark, occasionally blinded by the glare of headlights as someone's dad arrived home from work, frozen snow ruts crunching under the tires.

"Car," someone always shouted, and we parted like the Red Sea. Goaltenders dragged the nets aside, kids moved aside, waddling clumsily in bulky snowsuits, disappearing into roadside drifts taller than their toques. Then the game silently resumed until the final call for dinner resounded down the block.

We could afford only one kind of out-of-school lesson at a time. There weren't many choices, especially for girls. For a couple of winters Donna and I awakened our inner graces with weekly ballet classes. Later all three of us got a good grounding in reading music with piano lessons from Miss Lawrence, our beloved kindergarten teacher.

It was years before I realized some families couldn't afford any kind of after- school activities for their kids, or that everyone didn't have a summer cottage. My sheltered circle of friends didn't include anyone who went to a commercial summer camp. We had no idea what summer camps were like. The only ones I had ever heard of were the ones Dad told us about. He enthralled us with escapades from his university years of leading canoe trips at Taylor Statten's camps Ahmek and Wapomeo in Algonquin Park. "If that spoiled camper hadn't complained so much, I never would have had to accidentally tip her canoe."

Every time Mom served pie for dessert he'd say, "The only thing I learned at Camp Franklin in Georgian Bay was how to cut a pie in seven pieces."

I took for granted being surrounded by relatives who were ready, willing and able to teach skills needed to thrive independently, a great majority of the time alone with Mom on an island. All lessons were free, non-gender or age specific. Only two other kids in the lineup for rowboats and canoes.

Our parents encouraged us to entertain ourselves, develop skills and be independent. No TV, no tablets, no phones or computers, our summers centred on outdoor events. Despite having no TV at home, at an early age I got hooked on the idea of farflung adventures by watching TV at my best friend's house. Dad resisted buying a TV. "We don't need an idiot box in our house. CBC radio is enough for us." He didn't add that he didn't have the money.

During the school year Mom stood on the porch once a week to watch as I ran down the dark, snowy street to my friend Carol's house. *Ramar of the Jungle* aired on the black and white 16-inch television screen every Wednesday evening at 7 p.m. The hero of the series was Dr. Tom Reynolds, referred to by locals as Ramar, supposedly African for "white medicine man". Portrayed by American actor Jon Hall, Ramar reached remote jungle villages of Africa by dugout canoe. On lengthy trips up the Nile River he dispensed both medicine and good will. I was hooked. I wanted to be just like Ramar when I grew up.

One lazy hazy August afternoon that summer of 1953 my burgeoning canoe paddling skills serendipitously came together with my newfound obsession with the world of adventure programs. My overactive imagination coupled with my developing skills combined to instill a yearning for extended canoe trips.

Learning the fine art of canoeing seemed crucial to my future plans, third in line or not.

But, by 1953, Miss Niagara's decks sagged, her floorboards groaned under even my light step and water began to seep through her seams. Dad pronounced her destiny. "I guess it's time to retire the old girl."

His sad gaze reflected myriad tales of past adventures. That somber verdict made fierce competition for the privilege of rowing or operating Uncle Orie's motor in the rowboat.

Doug always vied to be first. "I need the boat to go fishing." In his mind he needed the boat every day.

"Okay. But, pick up some ice on your way home then. And, check the mailbox while you're there," Mom said.

Like Grandma, Mom didn't like being left on the island without a boat. Dad suggested a way to remedy the situation.

For several years Dad had coveted a red wood and canvas Peterborough canoe but felt he couldn't, or shouldn't, afford the

Dad in new red Peterborough canoe. —Will Shales

real thing, the original more expensive model. That spring he ordered a cheaper version, made in Quebec, from the T. Eaton Company. Sadly, when we got to the lake, the canoe had not arrived. Dad wasted no time heading for Charlie Hughson's store in Perth Road Village. "Can you make a call to Toronto for me? Our new canoe should have been delivered a couple of weeks ago."

Charlie nodded. Dad produced a scrap of paper with the number for Eaton's Toronto store and joined Charlie behind the counter. Charlie gave the phone a few vigorous cranks with the handle on the side of the wooden box.

"Yes, yes. I see. Okay. Just a minute."

It turned out the cheaper Quebec canoe was no longer available. Charlie relayed the message, then handed the phone to Dad. The conversation continued. When he replaced the receiver and turned to us, a smile brightened his face. "They say they'll send us a Peterborough canoe for the same price. And, we'll get two new paddles for our trouble. It'll arrive by train in a few days."

Lessons started with Doug a few days later. Dad sat proudly in the stern. Doug, a little more tentative, in the bow.

"Never let your paddle drag along the soft wood gunwales."

Doug frowned in concentration, paddle shaft rarely coming into contact with the gunwale. Donna and I knelt on the dock, paddles dipped in the water, imitating Doug's movements.

"Okay. That's good. Now you switch to the stern. We'll try steering with the J-stroke."

Donna got lessons next. Her gentle touch surprised us all. She was a natural. My lessons continued on the dock for several more days. The rough boards indented my knees, creating callouses. I didn't care. I knew in my heart I would have to be tough for the multi-day jungle river trips I planned. After what seemed an interminable number of days I earned a place in the bow seat. Dad manned the stern. My allotted time, usually less than half an hour, was never enough for me. After all, I was sure my future held grand adventures.

As the youngest, I was last to learn to paddle well, last to be allowed to venture solo out of sight of our granite foundation, the Front Rock. I longed to take the sleek new vessel out on my own, to show Dad how well I could manage solo, to make him proud of me. "Please, Dad. I'm old enough. I'm almost seven. I'll be careful."

After endless episodes of bargaining Dad relented, sort of. He tied one end of a twenty-foot painter rope to the stern of the canoe and the other end to the dock. My solo trips up the Amazon began.

The memory of my first 'extended' trip provided a foundation for strength and resilience. Because, shortly after I turned seven on August 12, one day I paddled Dad's cedar and canvas Peterborough canoe, alone, all the way up the Nile River. The oncoming current surged against the bow. The waves splashed her hull continuously. The relentless sun reflected blindingly off the water. My arms often grew tired, but I never gave up, I forged ahead, stroke after stroke, eyes on the river, for hours at a time. All on the end of a 20-foot tether.

I learned a lot about paddling that summer. I learned how difficult it was to paddle in a straight line, how to read the wind, how not to let your paddle scrape the side of the canoe and how great it was to have a dad that would rescue me and pull me back to the dock when I needed help.

That was the way it worked in our family. Mom and Dad gave all three of us lots of 'rope', fostered our resilience, but were always there to reel us in and provide love and support when the situation called for it.

One evening Dad sent Donna and me in the new canoe to pick up the mail at the farm. We paddled to shore, proud Dad trusted us. We stepped out of the boat in the shallow water at the Cedars' Beach before the keel touched the sand.

"Even if it's a short visit, never leave the canoe in the water close to the shoreline. A wind can come up suddenly," Dad cautioned.

Arms straining slightly, we lifted the canoe, waded ashore and gently upturned it on the grass. We ran all the way up the hill to the mailbox, waved briefly to cousin Mary and Aunt Alice, then bolted back down the hill. Carefully we waded back into the shallows, carrying the canoe. Donna steadied the stern while I stepped in. She boarded in the stern without tipping. Mom and Dad's trust and confidence in us to accomplish real tasks honed our growing skill and sense of responsibility. We knew they could see us from the island dock.

It wasn't long before we earned permission to travel briefly out of Mom's sight as far as Aunt Jessie's to pick up fresh bread. "You'll be out of sight past the point. No lollygagging," Mom warned.

It was a short fifteen-minute trip to Jessie's. We stepped out in the shallows and dragged the boat to shore below Jessie's farmhouse. Bubbles exploded, tickling our ankles, as the bay marsh sucked our bare feet down into the marl. It was easy to be distracted by the squish of clay between our bare toes. Digging in the muck for crayfish, snatching frogs and searching for baby turtles often made us late. Mom's yearning for Jessie's bread outweighed her annoyance. The scolding didn't last long. Every adventure added strength.

We loved fishing, swimming, rowing and paddling and being sent off island on errands. Some skill development wasn't as much fun. When Dad was expected on Friday evening, doing laundry became part of our list of necessary skills. Mom relied on us for help. She tried to make it fun. It didn't always turn out that way.

One sunny Friday morning Mom asked Doug to drag the square galvanized pail and washboard across the increasingly shallower swamp, thanks to Dad's landscaping. He placed it on the flat rock, the only solid surface in the swamp, steps from the swimming rock. Donna and I followed with the water pails, formed a bucket brigade and filled the tub with lake water. Mom poured in a minimal dose of powdered detergent from the red, yellow and blue Tide box, then handed it to Donna. "Take this back up to the cottage. Put it in the orange crate." She knew from experience when the soap powder got wet the fine granules adhered to each other to form crusty blocks.

Mom glanced skyward. "Keep your undies on. Everything else in the tub. Most of it will dry by tonight."

There wasn't much to do. Underwear and bed sheets mostly. I was assigned the undies and pillowcases.

"Go easy on the washboard. It's getting old."

I squatted in the grass, leaned into the tub, soapy water welled up past my elbows. Doug and Donna took their turn with the sheets.

"Time for rinsing."

One by one Mom carried armloads of soapy, dripping sheets to Front Rock. With only our immediate family in residence on the island there were six sheets in the pile. Donna and I shared a double bed. Donna and I each grabbed a corner and swam out to the deep, treading water while swishing our arms back and forth. The idea we could be polluting the source of our unfiltered drinking water never entered our minds. Mom stood to get a better angle on our progress.

"Don't come back in yet."

The tiniest trace of soapy water drifted away from the sheets. We had to tread water and keep swishing a little longer.

"Why do we have to do all the rinsing? Why doesn't Doug help?" Donna said.

Doug smiled sheepishly from where he sat in the laundry tub enjoying the warm sudsy water. At Mom's insistence he finally got out of the tub to help Mom and Donna wring out the sheets above the dry Front Rock. Twisting heavy flannel sheets in opposite directions was too much for me. I was so short the sheets dragged on the granite.

"Let's get these up on the line. They need to be dry by the time your dad gets here." An admirable 50s cottage housewife, Mom wanted clean sheets when Dad arrived for the weekend. "Doug, help Donna carry the tub up behind the cottage. Dump the soapy water in the woods away from the lake." It seemed a useless exercise after the way we had rinsed the sheets.

Friday before dinner I had the job of rowing the green rowboat to the landing on shore. Donna followed in the canoe. Doug stayed on the island, nursing a terrible rash. Too much leisurely lounging in the laundry tub.

"Serves you right for not helping us," I said. Secretly Donna and I felt sorry for him. We just didn't want him to know it. We left the rowboat for Dad and returned in the canoe.

After dinner, Roger, as he did instinctively every Friday we waited for Dad, sprawled into position on the end of the dock, gazing toward shore.

Doug in laundry tub at front swimming rock. —Eileen Jamieson

When Dad arrived at the lake on Friday night, he didn't want to leave again until Sunday evening. That Friday two circumstances cast a pall over his weekend. Just before bedtime Mom told Dad the bad news. "We'll have to go to the Corners in the morning to get some calamine lotion for Doug."

Then Dad shared his news. He pulled a letter out of his briefcase and laid it on the dining table, his expression somber.

"We got a letter this week from the Department of Lands and Forests in Tweed. They want us to pay for the island based on foot frontage for the waterfront all around the island." His words sounded hesitant, almost strangled. The lines on his forehead said it all.

This ridiculous notion of calculating waterfront all around the island frightened all of us. The calculated price added up to way more than our family could ever afford. The plaintive call of the loons sounded more melancholy than usual that night.

CHAPTER 14
ANCIENT VOICES

Early July 2006

"What do we do with the water when we're finished?" Natalie's long blond hair partially obscures her face as she bends over the collapsible pail. She swishes her laundry around in a circle of soapsuds. Claire, her paddling partner, stands close by, hands squeezing the last bit of soap out of her favourite T-shirt. We paddle our canoes into the landing area of Ancient Voices Wilderness Camp shortly after rafting our canoes for a floating lunch. This will be our last night of camping along the Yukon River.

Thunder and lightning temporarily forced us off the water earlier in the day. Now radiant sunshine welcomes us. An aura of mystical serenity and healing cocoons our motley crew. We found the site deserted but in true Yukon hospitality, hand printed signs inform us we are welcome to use the outdoor shelter for cooking and camp on the grass within the circle of log cabins.

There are fourteen of us: eight teenagers, four boys and four girls, three teachers and three parents, all from the Richmond District Incentive Program, an alternative school operated by the Richmond School District in BC. Under the leadership of the head teacher, my husband Barry Hodgins, we had been paddling the Yukon River for more than two weeks. We'll be in Dawson City tomorrow. Natalie and Claire have declared clean T-shirts a necessity for our triumphant arrival in the legendary gold rush metropolis.

"Take it up there into the woods. Find a spot where there's lots

Patti and Barry with the gang from Richmond, BC's District Incentive Program,
Ancient Voices, on the Yukon River. —Barry Hodgins

of soil and dump it there. Try to stay well away from the creek." I
point into the bush above the rustic wood sauna we stand beside.
I picture Donna and Doug hauling the laundry tub up the hill
behind the cottage. An Asian inspired split bamboo pole diverts
a trickle of freezing water from the nearby creek to the flagstone
terrace, a convenient platform for washing and doing laundry.

Once back at the camp we hang our laundry in the sun on lines
along the edge of the shelter. Thoughts of laundry day at the lake,
treading water and swishing sheets with Donna, Mom hanging
sheets in the sun.

Natalie, Claire and I reconvene on the patchy grass around the campfire circle, our backs to the outer ring of cabins. "Don't get me wrong. I'm looking forward to getting to Dawson City tomorrow, but I'll miss being on the river, for sure," Claire says.

Her alert eyes showed a depth of understanding well beyond her years. "What will you miss most?" I ask. Ever the teacher, I'm curious as to what she's thinking.

"I guess the simplicity of it all." She raises her right hand to brush her silky brown, no nonsense bangs from thoughtful chocolate eyes. "Nothing to worry about except cook breakfast, break camp, paddle all day, set up camp, make dinner and go to bed."

"No homework, no exams, no stress, no deadlines." Natalie says, gazing longingly off into the woods.

I have to agree. It's my first summer of retirement. No report cards to read, no schedules to create, no assemblies to plan. My gratitude encompasses the cottage camping and paddling skills that have led me to this place. This last three weeks have been all I ever dreamed of in my early days of paddling up the Nile in search of Ramar of the Jungle.

CHAPTER 15
INNOCENCE LOST

1953

Mom and Dad and their guests, new neighbours from Weston, pulled folding chairs up to the card table, ready for a game of bridge. Mom picked up the deck of Bicycle playing cards. She kept shuffling, over and over, her gaze slanted down at the table. After a prolonged silence Dad spoke. His back ramrod straight, the muscle in his jaw rigid, he looked directly into the eyes of Mr. Allen.

"Very sorry to hear you'll be leaving first thing tomorrow, right after breakfast." Mr. Allen returned Dad's gaze, at first quizzically, then rapidly followed by a startled expression of recognition. Dad didn't sound at all sorry.

"And, I guess you'll want to sleep in the tent tonight."

I didn't understand what was going on. Mom and Dad usually gave up their bedroom for guests.

"I think it's best if Anne and I sleep in the cottage tonight with the kids."

I had never heard him speak so curtly to anyone. Mrs. Allen directed a questioning look at her husband. She started to speak, eyebrows raised, then stopped herself. Head down, she concentrated on her hands, folded tightly in her lap. I didn't know what was happening. Something felt seriously wrong.

It had started out to be the perfect cottage day. Mr. and Mrs. Allen were the last guests of the season. Jamie had come in July,

Turtle rock, Loon Island. —Barry Hodgins

as usual, then in August Mom's sister, our Auntie Allison, with her family. Mom and Dad's friends from their bridge club, Gord and Eloise Montgomery and their family had rented the Cedars cottage on the shore for two weeks in August. Afternoons they spent playing croquet on our lawn and swimming from our granite rock base.

Mr. and Mrs. Allen and their son Billy, my contemporary at age seven, had arrived after lunch. As soon as they stepped out of the boat Doug, Donna and I corralled them to follow us on a tour along the path beaten by our bare feet around the perimeter of the island. Slabs of granite, bare of soil, protruding at various points along the shoreline defined the highlight locations. We started at First Rock, the flat piece of rock extending into the shallow water north of our cottage. When we started fishing Mom had declared it the perfect platform for cleaning fish. Dad taught us early how to clean fish. We lived by his rule. "You catch it, you clean it."

He was not a fisherman and didn't want to be involved. Mom

insisted we hurl the fish guts into the shallows well away from our swimming area. At dusk snapping turtles crawled up out of the marl like prehistoric relics to forage and feast on the tasty morsels. We told Billy we'd take him out after dinner to see if we could catch some turtles.

The tour around the tip of the island continued to a second smaller flat rock, almost inaccessible through dense cedar and birch trees. Second rock was a good spot for catching frogs, it didn't work for still fishing and we didn't have good rods for casting. The shallows extended, leaving the drop off to deep water farther away than the length of our bamboo poles.

The next stop along the path was Turtle Rock. Seemed we weren't the only ones who enjoyed soaking up the warmth of the sun from a granite platform. Countless generations of Draper Lake painted turtles claimed it as home base to saturate their shells with the required daily dose of Vitamin D3. The turtle Club Med comprised a grouping of six granite mounds, separated slightly over eons by pressures of winter ice. Every summer day around 4 p.m. the late afternoon sun crested our island. Rays warmed the grainy igneous surfaces. Each hillock became a mini turtle resort. Families of painted turtles, Toonie to platter-sized, wove their way through submerged water lily stems up onto rock to catch the rays.

Doug silently parted the bushes. Not a turtle in sight. "Too early. No sun on the rock yet," Doug explained. "Let's go to the Front Rock. I'll show you how to catch frogs."

Roger and I followed Doug and Billy. Mrs. Allen trailed beside us. "It's almost teatime. I'll go and give your mom some help."

Donna looked up at Mr. Allen. "Do you want to see our new tree fort?" Without waiting for an answer, she started along the path on the other side of the island on her own. Mr. Allen followed.

Back at the front of the island we found Dad was, as usual, thigh deep in water beside the dock. This summer's project necessitated pulling rocks out of the muck to shore up the stonewall defining the dock area. A half hour later the entire group gathered in front of the cottage for afternoon tea.

After dinner, as promised, we rowed Billy out to the drop off in front of First Rock for a turtle hunting expedition. Donna rowed silently, skillfully maneuvering the boat into position above the turtles' smorgasbord shallows. Doug reached down, picked up an unsuspecting reptile. Doug's thumb and middle finger just reached to either side of the algae covered hump of the shell. Dad had taught us this method of picking up turtles to avoid injury from the threatening beak and dinosaur-like triangularly crested tail. He placed the flailing tortoise on the floor of the boat next to Bill's bare toes. The frantic scratching of the turtle's claws on the wood floor of the boat must have spooked him. Muscles tensed, Billy leaned back on the middle seat. Just in time he lifted his bare feet out of range of the menacing jaws.

We caught four. Doug tried passing one to Billy. "I'm not touching that slimy thing. Get it away from me. It'll bite me."

We couldn't believe he'd never held a turtle. Even then we didn't realize the richness of the experiences we took for granted as every-day occurrences. He kept his feet up and hands on his knees the entire time. Mom called us in at dusk. Doug pulled the turtles from their hiding place under the peak seat and gently placed each back into the shallows. We watched as within seconds each dove, burrowed into the muck, and disappeared. Billy wouldn't put his toes down until all the turtles had disappeared into the depths. We felt a bit sorry for him being such a city kid. A musky scent permeated our nostrils, leaving the only trace of turtle presence.

Now pleasantly fatigued from an afternoon of island tours,

tea, swimming followed by dinner and turtle hunting, it was time to teach our guests our favourite family game, Matches.

The warm glow of coal oil lamps barely illuminated the four tattered cards in the centre of the table. The last of the orange and peach sky dulled as the moon rose slowly over the dark glimmer of the lake. The game started past our regular bedtime. Our adult guests sat at each the end of the table. The rest of us squished in along the long bench facing the lake. Dad's burgeoning carpentry skills had fashioned this long table from leftover siding boards. The table hung on hinges under the screened window facing the lake. When raised, two table legs swung down that could be fastened to stand upright with a sturdy hook and eye.

Mom mentioned the unstable conditions every time we played cards.

"It's certainly a step up from the cedar pole outdoor table. And, it's a great view of the lake. But, those coal oil lamps still make me nervous. Nobody jiggle the table."

Dad dealt the cards. He leaned forward from his camp chair behind me and whispered advice. I still needed help arranging the cards in my hand. A mound of burnt wooden match stubs sat in a pile beside my spot and everyone else's.

"Okay everybody. Anti-up," Dad said.

With varying degrees of dexterity, each player grabbed a fistful of match stubs from their pile. Fingers blackened from soot, they placed one match on each of the cards in the middle: Ace of Diamonds, King of Hearts, Jack of Spades and Ace of Clubs. I knew if I got to play one of the cards, I would win all the matches on the card. The other way to win was to play all your cards. Then you got to shout out, "I'm out. Pay me." When that happened everyone groaned, complained and had to pay you one match stub for every card left in their hand.

I learned counting, card suits, face cards, and how to borrow from the bank, an old tin full of match stubs, when I ran out. Mom and Dad willingly spent evening hours engaged with us in

Matches, Canasta, Snakes and Ladders and Chinese Checkers.

Thirty years later I discovered Matches was Dad's homemade version of Rumoli, a combination of poker and rummy, believed to have originated in Ontario in the 1870s. Somehow the game had found its way into our cottage traditions. Maybe Dad learned it from his Shales ancestors. Most people owned an official Copp Clark Publishing Company Rummoli board and a supply of red, white and blue plastic poker chips. We had neither. Instead, we had several large orange juice tins of blackened wooden matchstick stubs saved after lighting the kerosene cooking burners, coal oil lamps and campfires.

"That's it," Mom's pronouncement signaled the end of the game. "Nine o'clock. Time for bed for you kids. Everyone out. Show Billy where you brush your teeth, then go over the hill. Don't forget to wash your hands."

We filed outside to the washstand beside the cottage. Dad's handmade wooden cabinet had a top surface of painted boards holding a pail of water with a metal dipper beside a soap dish. As usual we fought over the toothpaste and jockeyed for position at the spitting rock. Billy waited patiently. An only child, he was definitely unschooled in the fine art of sibling rivalry. Playing host, as instructed by Mom, Doug grabbed his flashlight and guided Billy up the hill along the path through the dense cedars to our new two-holer outhouse.

Donna and I went next. Close behind on the path, I struggled to stay within the circle of light from her flashlight. I knew there weren't any bears. I'm not sure what I imagined loomed out there in the dark, but I stuck close, almost tripping on her heels, just in case. Back at the washstand we washed, pitched the soapy water off the spitting rock and went back into the cottage to say good night to our parents.

Dad had unhitched the legs and folded the dining table back against the wall. We found the four adults clustered around the card table. It was then, standing in the shadows, outside the circle of light that contained our parents that we witnessed the uncharacteristic, stiltedly awkward conversation. Mom obsessively shuffled the cards.

We went off to bed, Doug and Billy behind the partition at the end of the main room, Donna and I to the lumpy double bed we shared in the second new bedroom also partitioned from the main room. Not much later I heard Dad say, "I'm not feeling much like bridge. Let's call it a night." I heard the scraping of chairs, Dad folding up the card table and the slam of the screen door. Billy's parents headed for the tent. Mom and Dad settled in their bedroom. Troubled and puzzled by my parents' uncharacteristic lack of hospitality, I slept fitfully.

Early the next morning, following a silent breakfast, Dad rowed the guests to shore. No further explanation. They were never invited back.

Except for that uncomfortable weekend, it had been a great summer. Mom got her cottage kitchen that year, a six by ten-foot rectangle addition jutting out of the back wall, supported by cedar posts, leveled somewhat precariously by piles of flat rocks. Dad built a counter above two levels of open shelving that stored dishes and pots and pans along the back wall A screened window above the sink faced the woods. Grandpa's older brother, our great Uncle Jack, donated a white enamel sink that had once belonged to Aunt Hattie Shales, a distant relative, when she homesteaded in Frontenac Park, just north of the original Shales farms, in the early 1900s. A drainpipe emptied directly into the earth below the cottage. A pail for lake water with a dipper stood next to the sink.

We took turns doing the dishes with Mom. When I had the evening off, I sat in the crook of the rounded branch halfway up the big cedar tree close to the window. I could see through the dusty screen into the kitchen, through the cottage and out to the lake. I watched Donna fishing around with her hands in the Ivory Snow soapsuds. Doug stacked the dishes in the white plastic tray on the mottled gray and blue linoleum countertop. When it was his turn to wash, I stacked.

No gender discrimination. We all climbed trees, built forts, fished and cleaned fish, rowed, paddled, peeled potatoes and helped with the dishes. Our parents encouraged us to try new activities, new challenges, even if difficult at first. Their confidence in us created the foundation to pursue and overcome challenges later in life.

The old icebox stood at one end of the kitchen. Dad nailed the burners to the countertop at the other end. The awareness of the chance of fire and the devastation it could cause loomed large. "I'm afraid the burners could jiggle when your mother is cooking. We could burn down the whole island." I didn't want that to happen. Even then my entire identity consisted of being known as one of the Shales' kids from the island. Back in Weston I was demoted to Doug and Donna's anonymous little sister.

Dominated by Mom and Dad's yearning for simplicity or more likely because of a lack of funds, simple décor reigned. Compared to tenting it did feel like the lap of luxury. In the main room, two webbed folding green camp chairs faced two antique wooden rocker chairs Aunt Alice sent over from the farmhouse. Grandpa crafted a handsome coffee table from peeled cedar poles. He sanded and varnished the leftover smooth siding boards for a tabletop that glinted in the morning sun.

Dad thumbtacked a purple, silver and white University of Western Ontario pennant above a black and white photo of his alma mater's football team lineup, the Western Mustangs. Number 5, his number as a quarterback and star place kicker, became a number proudly worn by future generations of Shales soccer, hockey, basketball and volleyball players. Donna and I thumbtacked postcards from Kingston and Old Fort Henry above our bed. Doug put up hockey and baseball cards. Every summer it seemed more special, more our own, filled with mementos.

The 1953 Toronto winter dragged on like a cold, dark eternity. Elizabeth II was crowned queen of England's commonwealth in June, Louis St. Laurent won the federal election, and the Montreal Canadiens took the Stanley Cup. We constructed sturdy snow forts and staged wars with neighbour kids. Dad spent frigid evenings freezing a rink in the back yard. Despite frozen toes and fingers I was obsessed with learning to skate like our Canadian Barbara Ann Scott who had won Olympic Gold in women's figure skating in 1948.

One mid-winter bedtime Mom and Dad finally revealed the reality behind the abrupt departure of our previous summer's guests.

"Billy asked me to come over to his house after school tomorrow to watch TV. Can I go?" Mom tucked the covers around my chin. I could faintly hear Doug and Donna downstairs discussing math homework. We still didn't have a TV. I never wanted to miss a chance to watch Ramar of the Jungle. Episodes I had seen at my friend Carol's house had captivated my imagination. Once the seeds of wanderlust for exotic locales had been germinated, they continued to fuel my fascination for service in developing countries.

Dad wandered in from their bedroom next door. Mom told him what I had asked. "We don't think that's a good idea," he said. "It's okay to be Billy's friend. He's a nice boy. Best to play outside with him and not go to his house."

"Why not? I go to Carol's house all the time." This uncharacteristic response puzzled me.

"Billy came to the cottage. He's my friend."

Dad's voice lowered. He looked me straight in the eye. "Something happened when Billy's family came to the lake. It's not a good idea for you to go to their house."

Dad's back stiffened the way it had when he had spoken to Mr. Allen across the Bridge table. Mom cuddled me closer. "Do you remember last summer when you were showing Mr. and Mrs. Allen around the island?"

I nodded.

"Remember when Donna went alone with Mr. Allen to show him the tree fort?" The image of my eleven-year-old sister, blonde waves trailing down her back as she slipped off into the woods, followed by tall, dark-haired Mr. Allen popped into my head.

"Uh, hmm." I had no idea what Dad was getting at.

"Well, Mr. Allen pushed Donna down on the ground and tried to kiss her. She pushed him away and nothing happened."

I didn't really understand what that could mean. But, a bad feeling soured my stomach.

"Nothing else happened. Donna pushed him away." Mom's arm felt warm and protective around my shoulders. I knew that wasn't the way an adult should act. Instinctively I knew Mr. Allen's actions were wrong. Dad's words made me anxious. I squirmed under the covers.

Donna must have been confused and embarrassed after the incident. She hadn't said anything to Dad until he went to help her make up our bed after the game of Matches.

I remain in awe of the control it must have taken Dad to walk calmly back into the living room, face Mr. Allen and handle the situation in a controlled manner. Maybe his sensitivity to Mrs. Allen's feelings wouldn't allow him to throw them off the island in the middle of the night.

That's all Mom and Dad told me, except to assure me nothing else had happened. I pray nothing more happened to my beautiful, blue-eyed, innocent sister. The sanctity of our sacred place had been sullied, compromised by outsiders. For decades the island has kept our family close, given us strength, forged bonds of togetherness never to be severed. No one can take that from us.

Donna and I never discussed the incident, even as adults. I'm not sure why. Perhaps she buried it deep inside. I probably did, too. Maybe she preferred to obliterate that uncomfortable scene caused by a grown man she thought of as a trusted adult.

I didn't go to Billy's house. The family moved away the next spring. We never saw them again.

Mom and Dad rarely mentioned the possibility of losing the island. Even if they had, we would never have believed it could happen. As far as our family was concerned, we belonged on the island and the island belonged to us, just as Uncle Jack and Aunt Laura owned their island, Grandpa and Grandma belonged on theirs and Elwood and Alice were part of the farm. No dispute. The Shales belonged at Draper Lake, grounded by the granite. And Draper Lake would remain forever a part of them.

Later in the spring an official looking letter from the Department of Lands and Forests slid through the mail slot in our front door. Mom stewed about it all day, refusing to open it until Dad got home from the office. Before dinner they snuck off to their bedroom. Mom perched on the edge of the bed. Dad sat down at his desk. The three of us hovered near their slightly ajar bedroom door. Dad picked up his smooth redwood letter opener. He hesitated a moment as if making a wish, slit open the envelope, unfolded the paper and looked down. His shoulders sagged.

"The boys in Tweed just don't get it." Wearily he placed the offending dispatch back on the desk. "They still want us to pay foot frontage all around the island."

No one dared break the silence. Dad looked up. "I guess it's time to bring in the big gun lawyers at the office." By that time Dad had an executive position at the Canada Life Assurance Company in the head office in downtown Toronto. He was hopeful he'd find assistance from his colleagues.

CHAPTER 16
MATCHES

August 2018

*T*he warm glow of the overhead light barely illuminates the white plastic Rummoli sheet in the centre of our dining table. The dim lighting transports me to the past. I can feel Dad leaning over my shoulder, whispering instructions. The radiance warms me, conjuring the scent of coal oil lamps and excitement of childhood evenings spent playing Matches.

I'm the last of the three of us to have my own Loon Island cottage. Almost twenty-five years before, just weeks after a tornado ripped through cottage country, Barry had built us a one room bunkie, past Turtle Rock, at Third Rock, on what we then considered as the back of the island. Over a three-year period, we have worked together to add a dining porch, perfect for family dinners, card games and jigsaw puzzles.

"Okay. Everybody anti-up." I walk back into the main room of the cottage, pop a packet of Orville Redenbocker into the microwave and retrieve a bottle of summer rose wine from the fridge. Our guests Kevin and Lesley and their teen-aged sons Gabriel and Zachary, have come for our annual game of Rummoli. Long time friends of Donna and her second husband Art, they rent Donna's cottage every summer. We love having Kevin and Lesley on the island. Anyone who loved and valued my sister is okay by me.

Donna has been gone for three years. Island life isn't complete without her. I see her everywhere; at the Front Rock, swimming between islands, rowing past her dock and when I pass where the tree fort used to be.

Donna was first to build her own cottage. But first, she more than paid her dues. True to family tradition she and her first husband, Bruce, camped around the point of the island at First Rock. They crammed into a two-room tent with their four daughters. The old icebox was coaxed out of retirement and lashed to a tree. When too many rainy days in a row made tenting close to unbearable, the entire family dashed around the point to the shelter of Mom and Dad's cottage for an evening of warmth, camaraderie and, of course, a game of Matches.

I'm a late bloomer. Donna was early. Her first daughter Lori arrived when Donna was eighteen, followed in alternate years by Sherri, Rondi and Patti. I moved West to Vancouver in 1975 to pursue new adventures. Donna concentrated on raising her family in Kitchener, Ontario. In later years she completed her university degree part time. By that time Lori was also pursuing her post-secondary education. They sang in together in the university choir. Donna often hung out with Lori at the Faculty of Music.

"My friends all loved my super young, hip mom," says Lori.

For Donna, child rearing switched to university, then teaching, counseling and in retirement, work as a yoga instructor. In the early years the trajectories of our life paths catapulted us in diverging directions, keeping us a generation apart. Eventually Loon Island helped us find our way back to each other.

In July 1976 I arrived at the lake for a brief stop off. The week-long visit was a respite from a 16,000 kilometre road trip around North America in my Dodge pickup with younger pals, medical students Rich and Dave James. Donna and Bruce were building their own cottage. Years later Donna and Bruce divorced. She married a fellow teacher, Arthur. They travelled the world, keeping the cottage as a home base. In retirement Donna delighted in being the first to arrive at the lake every season and the last to leave. She and Art even tried, unsuccessfully, using their aluminum boat as an icebreaker, to cross to the island early one April. The magnetic attraction of time on the family island pulled we three siblings home every summer. Each year drew us closer together.

After seventy-two summers on Loon Island, early onset Alzheimers ambushed her. Art continued to love island life. He rented the cottage only to special friends like Kevin and Lesley.

Players dutifully distribute red, white and blue poker chips on the plastic sheet. I pour a glass of chilled sauvignon blanc for Lesley and one for myself. "I still miss Donna. It seems so strange to be here without her," Lesley says. She looks across the table and raises her glass. I don't need to say anything. We both know we're toasting Donna. Eyes damp, I raise my glass to meet hers.

July 2021

When reflecting on incidents that shaped our time at the lake and my childhood in general I recalled Donna's disturbing experience.

"Do you remember when the our neighbours, the Allens, came to the cottage one weekend and Dad sent them packing so abruptly after only one night?" I say to Doug. His face clouds with instant recognition, sadness and a touch of big brother anger.

"I do," says Doug. "It shouldn't have happened." But in true Shales fashion of discussing only positive memories and not speaking in depth about personal feelings, the conversation ends as we both stare off toward the lake, lost in thoughts of our treasured sister.

"I still miss her every day," Doug says.

CHAPTER 17
BELONGING

1955

With each new summer and every new experience our connection to the soil and granite of our island deepened and our sense of belonging to our extended family expanded.

My siblings and I were children of summer. Doug was born on July 30. Donna's birthdate, September 4, sadly heralded the end of summer, and even worse, the return to Toronto and the start of school. My birthday squished between the two, August 12. This year I had a perfect day planned. It was my last summer of single digits.

The morning started with a pre-breakfast dip. Mom, Donna and me, all in our birthday suits. Girls only. Doug and Dad stayed in the cottage. Next, I campaigned and won an extra pour of maple syrup on my porridge. After lunch I managed to whine my way out of my turn at dish duty. Instead, I climbed up and sat up in my favourite branch in the cedar tree behind the kitchen. I peered through the black screen to watch Doug and Donna washing and drying.

My day of privilege continued when I snagged first call to row us to the mainland for fresh ice. Up the hill, past the vegetable garden, we spotted Cousin Mary leaning out of the icehouse window. Doug clambered up the rickety wooden ladder. Working together they chiseled out a huge block, heaved it over

Elwood and Alice's farmhouse. —Barry Hodgins

to the window and pushed. As the frozen hunk hit the ground Donna and I hopped back just in time to protect our bare toes. Doug and Mary, each holding one handle of the iron ice tongs, hauled the weighty bulk around the corner of the farmhouse. They hefted it onto the back porch with a thud.

Each time I arrived at the farmhouse I felt welcomed. I sensed my identity as an integral part of the Shales clan, my heart somehow connected to the barren, rocky landscape. An invisible thread of unconditional acceptance tied me to past generations.

In 1886, my great grandfather, William Edward Shales and his wife Martha (Mary) Ann Ennis built a log house here for their growing family. Ten years later he built a two-story farmhouse. The stalwart Victorian, still painted white with forest green trim, oversees the lake from its grand hilltop position.

In those early years the view from William and Annie's bedroom focused away from the lake, toward the chores of the day. Work-related barn board outbuildings extended from both sides of the house to form a circle of self-sustaining farm life. The summer kitchen shared a wall with the main house. Across a narrow path two maples shaded the poorly-lit interior of the blacksmith shop, with an icehouse above. Packed in sawdust the ice lasted the entire year. Past the well, a triple-bay drive shed housed a winter sleigh, a stable for a team of workhorses and a carriage. A milking shed stood across the farmyard from the porch, adjacent to the chicken coup and the outhouse.

William later extended a pathway north about one hundred metres from the house and widened it to form a rudimentary track to accommodate wagons. After raising a new barn at the end of the roadway he installed two rows of milking stanchions, iron brackets that reached around the neck of each cow to secure them while being milked, for the growing herd of Holstein dairy cows. The malodorous scent of manure and eye-watering reek of barnyard urine vanished when the cows moved to the new milking spot. William also found a new home beside the barn for the chicken house, closer to the new barn, and added an adjacent pigsty.

William and Annie had six children in twenty years. Harold Merton, the eldest, died after WWII. My grandfather, William Elmo, and his identical twin, Walter Elmer; John Melville (known as Jack), and Elwood Spencer were all born in the log house. Baby Annie Louise arrived later in the Victorian house. William, Walter and Jack walked or occasionally road the farm horses to elementary school in Perth Road Village, about three kilometres away. They boarded in Sydenham to attend high school and finally graduated from Queen's University in Kingston with degrees in Science and Education.

As was the custom of the time, when Louise married Arthur Morley, she moved to his family farm. Elwood inherited the

Patti and Mary on the back porch of Mary's house 2021. —Barry Hodgins

Shales house and land along with the considerable responsibility of keeping the farm going. He courted and married Alice Jamieson and brought her home to Draper Lake.

By the time my ninth birthday rolled around only the well, the blacksmith shop, the icehouse and the drive shed still stood near the house. Elwood's tools festooned age- blackened interior boards of the drive shed. Clouded glass jars and rusted tins bursting with equally rusted used nails were crammed between hoarded bits of string and assorted washers. Elwood still used the original horse drawn carriage to transport cream to the cheese factory in Perth Road village. A sleigh remained in the adjacent bay. During spring, when sap flowed freely through maple veins, the cutter hauled brimming cans of sap to the shack in the middle of the sugar bush on the edge of the farm property. The clear sap was then dumped into a shallow metal pan to be reduced to syrup above a fire that was kept roaring day and night.

From the porch the view of pink and purple blossoms of Aunt Alice's morning glory vines almost obscured the still operational outhouse, which slanted slightly in place next to an energetic jungle of raspberry bushes. Past the raspberry canes, a field of ripening corn stood tall in the glare of mid-August sunshine.

When the ice thudded on the porch, Aunt Alice looked up, abandoned her broom, swiped her hands on her flour and berry-soiled apron and walked into the farmhouse kitchen. The ubiquitous summer slap of the screen door announced her entrance. Intoxicating aromas emanated from the interior. Juicy peach and raspberry pies sat cooling on the counter in the pantry. Several pans of fluffy buns, tanned to perfection in the wood stove, gleamed with a butter topping. In the main kitchen golden strips of flypaper, sticky with carcasses, swirled above the dining table.

In perpetual motion, patience personified, her own chores completed early, Alice willingly embraced the task of fulfilling my birthday wish. She stepped back out to the porch carrying a large wooden bucket containing the ice cream churn and an empty metal bucket. Under her arm she brandished a threatening-looking ice pick. About 30 cm long, the sharp instrument had a pointed metal spike attached to a worn wooden handle. We took turns caving slivers of ice off the block and transferring them to the bucket with our bare hands. By the time we filled the bucket our fingers were freezing.

"Okay. I think it's time to start. Pack as much ice as you can down in the space between the outside wooden bucket and the inside container. The cream's already inside. Check the lid. Make sure it's screwed tight." Alice surveyed the action, hands on hips. We sat on the porch, legs dangling over the edge.

We took turns rotating the stiff crank, a job that seemed endless. Alice periodically checked our progress. "You're going to need more ice."

Elwood and Mary beside the drive shed circa 1946. — Courtesy of Mary Newport

Doug and Mary disappeared around the corner to the icehouse for another block. When they returned Aunt Alice produced another equally lethal looking implement from the pantry, this time a knife as long as her beefy forearm. She handed it to Mary and looked at me. Since childhood I have secretly harboured an unfathomably heightened fear of sharp instruments. Even today, involuntary shivers ripple my spine at the mere thought of the shining stainless steel blade of a Swiss Army knife.

"Would you like some glads for your birthday? They're early this year." Gladiolas, my birth flower, soared elegantly along the back of Aunt Alice's vegetable garden. She always remembered my birth flower. I got to choose my favourite colours; white, pink and purple. Mary did the cutting. A seasoned farmhand, she used all tools with equal ease.

"Elwood needs you kids up at the barn," Aunt Alice called out the pantry window. "I can see him waving. Go on up and see what he wants." We trouped after Mary toward the barn. We found Uncle Elwood beside the swinging gate of the pigsty cavorting in circles, one tattered overall strap flapping over his bare shoulder. Shirtless in the August humidity, matted, sweaty chest hair curled over the top hem of the overalls. His black rubber boots coated in churned up barnyard mud, he frantically tried to corral the entire bumper crop of twelve-week-old piglets.

"I'll give you ten cents for every one you catch," Elwood shouted, eyes glued to one of the nine dusty pink sausage-shaped prizes. We joined the fray, bare feet smoothly slipping through puddles of mud and urine, glissading like mountaineers across a snowy slope. We grabbed them by their curly tails, their back legs or wrapped our arms around their portly middle sections. Faces speckled with mud, we hauled them squealing back to the sty. I don't remember ever being paid for our trouble. Uncle Elwood paid us in fun times and inclusion in farm activities and by daring us to venture out of our suburban comfort zone. He expected us to do everything Mary could do. Of course, we couldn't measure up to Mary's skills. Elwood challenged us just the same.

Skills for island living were one thing. Surviving on the farm, another. Before we left that day/that summer, Elwood invited me to try my hand at milking one of his Holstein dairy cows. "Pull up a stool beside me. Give me your hand." Elwood placed my tentative fingers under his on the cow's teat. "Just squeeze and pull. See?" Squishier, yet rougher textured than I expected, the teats felt like elastic bands grown less pliable with time.

His hand squeezed over mine. Embarrassed to be entering into such an intimate relationship with a cow I barely knew, I reluctantly allowed my hand to remain under his. When Elwood yanked, streams of pale white liquid pinged the bottom of the metal pail. When I pulled on my own, nothing happened except the swat of the cow's tail. She turned with a glare of impatience at the owner of the novice hands. A few more unproductive pulls produced more impertinent stares and tail swishes to my head.

I picked up my stool and moved away, preferring to watch from what I considered a safe distance. "Come a bit closer. Open up." With the ease of a trained marksman Elwood turned the teat, pulled and squeezed. Bull's eye. The well-aimed stream coated the back of my throat. Warm milk dribbled down my chin onto my T-shirt.

Basic milking was one thing. But the mysteries of milk and cream production truly eluded me. At home in the city, milk magically materialized from a red and white Carnation Instant Non-Fat Dry Milk box. Frugal to a fault, Mom scooped the requisite number of spoonfuls into a clear glass milk pitcher, added tap water then one of us stirred the pale whitish-blue liquid until the so-called "magic crystals" dissolved. We hated powdered milk straight. Every second or third day the sound of glass bottles clinking in a Silverwood's Dairy metal basket announced the arrival of our milkman. Sam delivered two or three bottles of whole homogenized milk to the small cubbyhole set into the red brick wall by the side door of our house. Mixed with the powdered concoction our milk became more palatable. On special occasions, like Christmas or Thanksgiving, Mom splurged on pints of cream for coffee or whipping cream to top her homemade pumpkin or mincemeat pies.

I always felt a bit hard done by when I was invited for dinner at my best friend Carol's house. He mom casually poured our milk directly from a bottle that had been delivered to her door.

At the farm cream and homogenized milk were plentiful. Aunt Alice, the undisputed queen of cream production, reigned at the separator. She carried water boiled on the woodstove in the farmhouse kitchen to the barn and sterilized every millimetre of the separator. After covering the large metal separator bowl with cheesecloth, she clipped it in place with wooden clothes pegs. Mary and Elwood hand milked the cows, then poured the milk through the cheesecloth into the separator bowl. Alice turned the attached wheel to keep the bowl rotating. Centrifugal force caused the lighter buttermilk particles to rise to the top. Heavier skim milk settled to the bottom. The cream flowed down the higher spigot into a five-gallon can. Milk slipped down the lower tube into buckets. Once several large cans were filled with cream, Elwood lowered the sealed cans by rope into the well in the barnyard to stay cool. Once a week he hauled them out, loaded them on the wagon and delivered them to the cheese factory in Perth Road Village. Some milk went to the dining table. Elwood mixed the rest with feed for the pigs or the weaned calves.

A while later we clambered back onto the porch.

"Almost time for testing," Aunt Alice called through the pantry window.

The muscles in my right arm strained to give the handle of the ice cream churn one more crank. Hands full with a small pitcher of maple syrup and a bowl of fresh wild blueberries from the far edge of the farm's acreage, she joined us on the porch. The screen door slammed behind her as she placed the berries and syrup beside the ice cream churn, plopped herself into the weathered porch rocker and smoothed her faded housedress across her knees.

I am ashamed to admit we considered her a bit of a country bumpkin. We cringed when she said, "Fiddle-dee-dee," while sweeping the porch for the umpteenth time. Alice witnessed life through unfashionable bottle-thick glasses, didn't seem to care much for her appearance, and wore ankle socks with sandals just like Aunt Hazel. But with Aunt Alice we were willing to overlook this obvious fashion faux pas. Her kitchen door was always open. Spending time with Alice offered a bounty of warmth, patience and unconditional acceptance as extended family. Frumpy or not, she made us feel special.

Dad once told me Alice had graduated at the top of her class at the high school in Sydenham, a village fifteen kilometres south of Perth Road. I wondered whether her lot as a farm wife fulfilled her. Did she have other dreams beyond the endless toil of preparing meals over the heat of the woodstove, hauling heavy pails of water from the well and hand-mending work clothes? She spent summer days harvesting row upon row of carrots, potatoes, tomatoes, peas and onions then canning produce for the winter.

"Now unhook the hand crank, gently, like I showed you last time."

Donna helped me open the top and lift the paddles. As it was my birthday, Aunt Alice passed me a spoon for the much anticipated first taste. I dipped, licked and looked up. Perfection.

"Do you think it's ready to add the syrup and berries?" Alice asked. I nodded. Alice rocked her chair forward for a closer look. "Okay, pile in the syrup and berries. Then give it a few more turns to mix them."

My arm still ached but the privilege of having Aunt Alice's heavenly concoction of cream and farm fresh eggs with wild

blueberries and maple syrup for my birthday outweighed any
level of pain.

A while later when Charlie Hughson drove into the yard to
deliver the mail, I ran to meet him. Out of the truck window he
handed me a birthday card from my new best friend, Karen. Her
family had a cottage at Balm Beach, a small cottage community on
Georgian Bay. I lived in a small world in Weston in winter. Carol
moved away when she was ten. Now Karen was my one best friend.
No wonder I thought everybody had a cottage.

We thanked Aunt Alice, before Mary and Doug, then Donna
and I, took turns lugging the churn down the hill to our rowboat.
Mary jumped in, too. She was coming for dinner. I mustered my
remaining energy to claim the rower's seat for the return trip to
our island.

The spicy aroma of Mom's homemade spaghetti sauce with
meatballs wafted toward us as we approached the island. Shortly
before dinner cousin Kenny arrived, his feet still soaked from
walking through the swampy area between our two islands that
we called 'No Man's Land'. He presented me with a card and
present, supposedly from my cousins Kenny and David, but
in reality, from their mother, my Aunt Gladys. Aunt Gladys
had two sons, but she longed for daughters. Aunt Gladys wore
dresses and skirts at the lake. We considered her elaborate attire
impractical, especially when stepping in and out of boats. In
contrast, most days Mom wore shorts and Dad's old plaid shirts
with the sleeves cut out.

Donna and I remained secretly in awe of Aunt Gladys. And,
we loved her. She always remembered our birthdays. I undid the
luxuriously thick ribbon decorating the parcel wrapped in
shiny paper to discover copies of *Elle* and *Vogue* magazines. I
guess Gladys held out hope I might someday become less of
a tomboy. Well-intentioned and meant with love, the glossy
images didn't interest me.

Finally, from the kitchen, the magic words, "There they are. Right on time. Spaghetti's ready. Somebody go give Grandma and Grandpa a hand at the dock."

After dinner Dad arranged camp chairs on the lawn tightly circled around the ice cream churn. "Get a move on everybody," Dad said. "The ice cream is melting fast." Mom brought out the metal scoop, spoons and bowls. She scooped. I distributed. She reminded me to serve Grandma and Grandpa first. A light breeze across the front lawn dispersed the last few mid-August mosquitoes.

From the Front Rock we could see the white farmhouse blushing under a rising crescent moon. The sky switched from pastel pink to fiery orange. Female fireflies flickered in the grass around our feet and frolicked into the forest behind us, lighting their tails to signal their readiness to mate. Some flew over the marsh along the edge of the lake, their reflections soaring to greet the stars. Cocooned by family, enveloped by the security of our island retreat, a birthday to savour. No mention of ominous letters, land issues or foot frontage prices.

Our guests departed, then last thing before bed we undressed and laid our pyjamas out on our beds. Then, wrapped only in towels, all five of us scampered in a row through the dark, barefoot across the damp grass to the Front Rock, dropped our towels on the granite and slipped into the ebony silk of the lake in our birthday suits, giggling with delight. When we had company on the island, Mom insisted on boys and girls swimming separately after dark. When it was just the five of us, a family skinny dip was the perfect way to end a birthday celebration. We turned onto our backs to float under the stars. Roger remained on the rock, his eyes glowing red with concern.

Later, loon calls lulled me to sleep.

CHAPTER 18
BIRTHDAY PLANS

May 2021

"*Oh, Patti. Hi. So good to hear from you." Doug's wife, my sister-in-law Margo, has a knack for making me feel like she loves receiving a call from me.*
"*Is Doug there?*"
"*No. He's at the cottage.*"
"*Good. It's you I want to talk to.*"

I tap the speaker button and place the phone on the dining room table beside my current jigsaw challenge, "Old Growth Forest of the Pacific Northwest". SilverStar Mountain has closed for the season but there's still lots of snow on the ground. I hope this puzzle will keep me going until time to hit the road East across Canada from British Columbia.

"*We're definitely coming. I've booked all the hotels. If all goes well, we'll arrive at the lake June 28." There's a cold knot in the pit of my stomach when I think of being turned back at the Ontario border due to Covid-19 restrictions. "I hear they're waving cars through if they have an Ontario license plate. The irony is we have a car with Ontario plates, but it's in storage in Ontario.*"

The Covid-19 pandemic kept us from the cottage last summer. Most of Canada on periodic lockdowns, non-essential travel was discouraged. We were afraid to step on a plane. Stuck at home at SilverStar Mountain Resort, I tried to make the best of it. But, gardening at altitude and paddle boarding on huge Okanagan lakes riddled with powerboats just didn't cut it. I'm spoiled, I know.

My life is divided between winters at a ski resort and summers on a private island in a quiet lake. It's the luck of the draw. Born into the Shales family I am bursting with gratitude. I take my responsibility as a steward of Draper Lake seriously. Now, more than ever. Doug will be eighty in July. Me, I'll be seventy-five in August.

My heart is calling me home.

"I'm thinking of booking the patio at the Opinicon for Doug's birthday. Visions of family picnics at Chaffey's Locks down the hill from the lodge flood my mind. "I'll call and see if they'll reserve us a spot in case patio dining is open by the end of July."

Twenty-three kilometres from Draper Lake the stately, historic Opinicon Lodge, recently upgraded, teems with childhood memories. As kids we never entered the actual dining room. Too expensive. But, a visit to the ice cream parlour ranks right up there with time on the back porch at the farm and the taste of Aunt Alice's homemade vanilla with syrup and blueberries.

"I know he'll say he wants hot dogs and fruit cocktail." My brother is a stickler for tradition. It's what he wanted for his birthday supper for as long as I can remember. A large family gathering at The Opinicon would never be his first choice.

"Some things never change."

Turns out two of their three children are able to attend. Their son Dean and daughter Drue will arrive from Oakville, Ontario with their spouses. Covid restrictions will prevent Kerry from bringing her family from Los Angeles.

Margo describes the menu. "Dean will barbecue Doug's favourite sausages. Drue will bring a salad. And, Dean's wife Beth will make the traditional Shales birthday cake, Betty Crocker's Midnight Chocolate layer cake with White Mountain frosting, just the way your mom used to make it."

"Sounds perfect. What can I bring?"

"I'll call the kids and get back to you. Don't say a word," Margo says.

CHAPTER 19
THE HIGH WATER BOYS

1953

Dad's tall silhouette loomed large, a ghostly shadow in the doorway of the bedroom I shared with Donna.

"Interested in a little adventure?" Dad whispered before dawn early one Sunday in July. "Sweater and long-sleeved shirt. No bare feet." Dad forever harped on that rule about sensible shoes. "Grab your bamboo pole and tackle box."

I didn't think we were going fishing. Dad hated fishing. But, I kept quiet. Whatever his reason for asking me to bring fishing gear, I didn't care. I loved spending time with him. When it was just the two of us, it made me feel special.

Suitably attired, sneakers laced, I slipped past Doug's bedroom and out the door and crossed the dark, needle-strewn dirt to the dock. Proceeding gently to avoid slipping on the dewy boards, I stepped into the rowboat. Without invitation Roger leapt in after me and assumed his usual figurehead position on the bow peak. I settled in the stern seat as Dad pushed off. He lifted the oars, soundlessly dropped the pins into the oarlocks and began to row.

"Why aren't you starting the motor?"

"Shush. We don't want to wake anyone." Mom knew we were going. There were never any secrets between Mom and Dad.

I thought he was being considerate of others around the lake who liked to sleep in. Later I discovered there was more to the story.

The oars barely rippled the pre-dawn stillness of the lake. I hugged my sweater close against the chill. Roger lifted his head to sniff the morning. Like a spy leading a covert mission, Dad rowed smoothly away from our island. When we rounded the point past Grandpa and Grandma's island he lifted the blades of the oars above the water and hesitated. Droplets glistened in the early rays of sun, then plopped into the lake, creating concentric circles. He turned to peer over his shoulder at the distant shoreline, took a visual reading on his destination, turned back and pulled on the oars.

"Are we going to Aunt Jessie's for bread?" The timing didn't seem right. We usually went in the early afternoon.

"Gives Jessie some time to cool the bread a bit," Mom always said.

The boat glided along in full view of Aunt Jessie's kitchen window. I had no idea where we were going. I didn't know of any other cottage or good fishing spot in that part of the lake. Dad continued his vigorous effort, the hull swiftly skimming the surface past their cabin. Was he trying to avoid Aunt Jessie's prying eyes?

When we reached the shore, he shipped the oars in front of a wall of reeds. The boat drifted, then gently nosed into a narrow opening, almost concealed by bulrushes. Red-winged blackbirds flitted away to hide in the canopy of poplars. A great blue heron indignant we had disturbed its serenity, squawked his disapproval. He flapped noisily away in search of a quieter locale. Roger flinched when a kingfisher swooped down past his head heading for a dive among the lily pads in pursuit of crayfish.

"You take the rower's seat. I'll go in the stern," Dad said. He stood and picked up the slim cedar pole we used for pushing off the shore. "Saves the oars." Without explanation he poled the boat further into the bulrushes, aided by a barely discernible current.

"Where are we going?"

Statuesque in the stern, Dad poled us ahead like a skilled gondolier. "This is the only outlet in the lake. It leads up to that bridge we cross before the road gets to Aunt Jessie's place."

"But, why are we here?"

"We're just going to have a quick look under the bridge to check how the water's flowing out of the lake. Our front lawn is still too squishy for badminton. I didn't dredge and shovel all that marl for nothing. Your mother likes a dry lawn for afternoon tea." He leaned his full weight into the pole.

Rushes grazed the gunwales of the boat. I spotted two green leopard frogs lolling on lily pads. Dad focused straight ahead. I decided it was better to wait to snag a couple on the way back.

Within site of the bridge, Dad shoulders tensed. "The buggers have been at it again." Dad never swore in front of kids. This was new and sounded serious. I wasn't sure who he was talking about.

He yanked on his high rubber boots, jammed his hands into his torn work gloves and stepped out into the shallow water. I stood up and watched. Each footstep disturbed the black mud. Bubbles rose to the surface, closely followed by the rich stench of bygone forests. Closer to the bridge he paused, placed his hands on hips and surveyed the situation. "Somebody tossed some cement blocks under the bridge."

Twigs, dead leaves and other detritus had snagged on them, all stemming the outgoing flow of water. "Must have been the High Water Boys." He leaned down and started hefting blocks and swinging them up on the bank.

On the thousands of lakes scattered over Canada's vast wilderness, the range of opinions about preferred water levels has always roughly equalled the number cottagers. Our lake was no exception. The fact that in those early days ninety-nine percent of Draper Lake owners were members of our extended family made our situation stickier than most.

When John Harbor Shales and his wife Mary Thomas first settled on the shore of the lake, the level was much higher. John and Mary ran a sawmill in the creek near the outlet to mill lumber from their own trees to build their home. The dividing line between our island and Uncle Dave's was underwater. The first three generations of Shales would never have imagined the frivolities of canoeing, camping and building summer cottages on islands. They harvested the straight, stately island pines, floated them back to shore then ran them through the outlet creek sawmill to create boards for their homes, barns and outbuildings.

By the late 50s, the sawmill long since dismantled, the lake level had naturally lowered. Dad had mixed feelings about the water level. His opinion depended on whether he had to pay for our island based on foot frontage of waterfront or by acre. Still engaged in a furious round of correspondence with the Department of Lands and Forest, he knew if he had to pay for the island according to foot frontage, it was better to have it measured at the beginning of the summer. The cost would be lower if the lake level was higher, exposing less shoreline to be measured. He inquired in a lengthy letter, asking when they would send someone to survey and measure. He hoped to put them off until the following May. Early season, as early as possible. Get it done so he could continue to secretly facilitate a lower water level later in the season. While he waited for a response, he bowed to Mom's request for a less spongy badminton court and tea terrace.

Uncle Walter, Grandpa's twin, favoured high water. The rocky shoreline in front of his mainland cottage sloped gently into the lake. High water made it was easier for him to dock his boat. His son Keith agreed. Dad agreed with our grandpa. Grandpa's own island was small and he needed low water to give him more room to dock his rowboats. The feud continued, twin brothers and cousins stubbornly agreeing to disagree. The taboo subject remained unacknowledged in polite company. According to local rumours, Walter and Keith regularly pitched all manner of junk and old construction materials over the bridge into the creek by night. Dad cleared it before dawn.

Roger scampered in circles, tail wagging. Drunk with freedom from his ten-month backyard city enclosure he leapt in front, sniffing and nosing his way through twigs and branches. Despite his untrained suburban nose, he sensed a foreign scent. He stopped, rigid. His fluffy tail quivered. Dad threw one last block up the bank, leaving an empty spot. He reached in with his hand and pulled out a tangle of birch branches. That meant only one thing. Beavers. In our lake. Damming the outlet. "Damn." His head down, Dad's lips barely moved. Another swear. Now he sounded really serious.

"Whose side are they on?"

My soft-hearted Dad would never dream of harming a living thing. More than once on an evening paddle he steered us toward the beaver lodge close to the mainland shore behind our island. "The beavers will be out soon. Maybe we'll get a look." Slipping along the surface he directed the canoe in to give us a closer look at the lodge. While we waited, canoe drifting silently through the dusk, he whispered tales of Grey Owl, the British-born writer and conservationist who disguised himself as a First Nations man. "Maybe we should invite the beaver kits to live in the cottage with us, like Grey Owl did," Dad said.

I doubted entertaining beaver kit houseguests would work for us. Mom wouldn't even let Roger into the cottage, except during the worst thunderstorms.

However, while Dad considered harming animals off limits, he had no reservation about tearing apart their previous night's work. "They'll just have to build a dam somewhere else." Head ducked in concentration he untangled branches and flung them up the bank. "Their lodge is deep enough in the water. The kits are safe as it is." Using the boat pole as a lever he wiggled another white barked branch free, lifted it and heaved it out of the way. "Don't want to encourage them to cut anymore young birches." He straightened, palms supporting his lower back.

Elbows stretched back he took a last look.

"That'll have to do for now. Time to get out of here before Walter and his crowd drive by on their way to church."

Dad poled the boat back through the rushes. From my position in the stern I stretched out to scoop up a couple of unsuspecting frogs. I dropped them into an empty milk carton left from our last fishing expedition and closed the flap. Patches of luminous water lilies, coaxed open by the warmth of the sunrise, greeted us where the creek widened into the lake.

Exhausted by furious beaver sniffing escapades, Roger curled up on the floor at my feet. Dad set the oars and swiveled the boat toward home. About then we spotted Uncle Walter. "He's heading in our direction. Get out your fishing pole. Hook one of those frogs on you caught," Dad said.

Dad pulled hard on his right oar, lining the boat parallel with the weedy drop off. Sensing his urgency, I scrambled for my bamboo pole. With the unfeeling ruthlessness of a keen fisherman, I hooked the squirming frog under the chin. The barb split the skin easily and protruded out through its head. "This is a good spot. Quick. Drop your line."

Uncle Walter's boat, propelled by his small outboard, speedily approached. I watched the frog wiggle pathetically as the lead weight dragged it down into the weeds.

Uncle Walter eased his boat alongside ours. "What are you two up to?"

Finally I realized why Dad had told me to hurry and get my line in the water. "Nothing much. Patti wanted to try a little early fishing." Roger looked up, his expression innocent, muddy paws hidden. "How about you?"

"I'm off to Will's island to see if he and Spray want a ride to church."

With no phones in any of the cottages, an in-person visit was the only way to communicate. The thick lenses of Uncle Walter's glasses distorted the view of his eyes, making it difficult to tell what he was thinking. His lips curled in a sort of smile.

"Good luck with your fishing." He pushed off from our boat then tugged the cord on his Johnson motor. No luck. He gave it a second hard yank. The motor sputtered, then started. He pushed in the choke, turned his head and was gone.

Even after Walter's boat disappeared around the point, Dad insisted I keep my line in the water. "A while longer. Don't want to start any trouble."

I felt important, proud of my part in the morning's expedition, keeping the water low and our secret close. Slipping along toward our granite home base, my heart swelled with pride. I was worthy of Dad's trust, built within the bounds of our tight-knit family, grounded by the solid foundation of our island home.

CHAPTER 20
TEMPORARY TRUCE

July 2021

*B*arry and I propel our stand up paddleboards toward Doug's island. Skirting the perimeter of the lake we skim the surface, searching the shallows for turtles. It feels like walking on water. I'm hunting the legendary snapper who lives on the mainland shore opposite Doug's island. With a shell three feet across, it's easy to spot. I usually catch a glimpse of it at least once every summer. No luck this time, we turn toward Doug's island to see if he's up yet. We love the serenity of paddling first thing in the morning.

As we approach Doug walks out of the woods. He steps out on to his stationary dock lying safely above the water's surface.

"Your dock looks good this year." About a decade ago the water was much higher in the spring. "Remember that year a beaver tried to build a lodge under your dock?"

"How could I forget?"

"How did you get rid of it?"

"I'll never tell." But, like father, like son, Doug somehow got rid of the lodge without harming the beaver.

Today I wonder how the water magically sits at the perfect level for Doug's dock. The lawn at the Front Rock at Mom and Dad's original cottage is dry enough for badminton so early in the season.

Like messages in the old circle game of telephone, rumours become garbled and take on a life of their own when filtered through several generations. "Dad told me somebody once installed a cement abutment to curb the outflow of water," I say.

Doug looks up. "Yeah. I heard that one, too. He also told me someone else blasted it out."

First Doug tries to tell me none of that is true. Then he says, "I don't know who it was. And, I wouldn't tell you if I did."

Although the original gentlemanly combatants are now long deceased, the water level dispute continues from time to time, in various forms. After all, tradition is tradition. Luckily for my patriarch brother, several newly arrived mainland cottage owners tend to be Low Water Boys. Consecutive generations of opponents have mellowed, some. Self-recruited volunteers have swelled the ranks of early season and occasional Sunday excursion battalions.

Doug smiles. I can tell I'm about to hear another secret. "Recently someone who shall remain nameless trapped a beaver in the creek. When they couldn't get it out of the trap they called the authorities for help. The wildlife officers were not amused." Doug leans forward, offering this nugget of confidential information in a whisper. He is well aware of how easily voices carry over water. I was glad to hear the beaver now swims free and the perpetrator was given a serious scolding.

Summer unfolds as always. Badminton racquets still swing above a pleasantly dry lawn, followed by raucous rounds of competitive croquet. Winners celebrate victories over ceremonial high teas. And, the front lawn is dry enough for campfires. As darkness takes over, it's easy to glimpse a beaver scooting along the drop off of the Front Rock.

Here on Loon Island summer rituals stand sacrosanct.

CHAPTER 21
OFF ISLAND
1955

Roger noticed first. Shortly after breakfast Dad donned his faded paint-stained plaid shirt with the rip at the elbow and changed into a clean shirt with a collar and long pants. Then Mom emerged from their bedroom in clean shorts and a halter top. Roger scampered down to the dock and into the rowboat. He sensed something was up. Maybe down on his level he easily spotted everyone except Mom was wearing shoes. Determined not be left behind he lay sprawled in the bottom of the boat and waited patiently for the rest of his family. He sensed our imminent departure. What he didn't know was our destination—the abandoned lead mine on the far shore.

We had tried leaving him in the cottage alone when we left the island. His incessant, plaintive bark followed us across the water, haunting our hearts.

"He sounds so sad," Donna said.

"And, so worried," Doug said.

"Why can't he come with us?" I asked.

We had tried leaving him free outside when he was a small puppy. That didn't work either. He swam after us. Once Dad rowed halfway to the mainland before we noticed his beige and white fluffy head frantically waving back and forth above the surface, searching for a glimpse of the family he thought to be deserting him. Panicked, we demanded Dad do something.

"Dad. Turn around. Please. He'll drown. Please." Our chanting convinced Dad.

He maneuvered the oars to pivot the boat, rowed back to meet Roger and hauled him over the side. Exhausted and wet, Roger shook not once, but twice, soaking us all. Then he snuggled happily at Mom's feet. From then on we included him on all family outings.

Once settled in early July we rarely left the island. While Dad worked in Toronto most of the summer, we entertained ourselves with excursions close to home. Most forays found us paddling or rowing to other family islands or sticking long cedar poles on the edges of sandbars and spits to tie the rowboat to prevent it from drifting away from our favourite fishing spots. Occasionally we ventured a short walk from the shore past Grandpa's island to gather flaky clumps of mica from the rim of one of two abandoned pit mines.

"Don't go too close to the edges," Mom said.

Mom imagined we might slip on the loose gravel at the edge of the pit and never be seen again. We snuck close enough to call out our names, close enough to hear them returned, echoing from the mysterious, rocky depths. Back at the cottage we used our fingernails to peel the thinnest flaky layers of mica possible. We marvelled at how this brown filmy substance had once served as windows for local pioneers.

The last thing Dad wanted after the five-hour drive from Toronto on a Friday night was to interrupt his weekend with a family outing. Based at the lake full time, we craved a bit of variety. When Dad joined us for his holidays, he succumbed to pressure.

Once every summer Dad gathered the troops for the lengthy, grueling, uphill hike to the site of the abandoned lead mine. Mom and Roger stayed at the island. Mom needed a break, some time to herself. Dad deemed the mine too dangerous for Roger. Who knew what he might step on or fall into.

"Long sleeved shirts, long pants, socks, shoes and hats, everyone.

There's poison ivy all over the trail."

Somehow he always managed to choose a sweltering, humid day. Despite leaving the island right after breakfast, we sweated along the trail. Perspiration stained the back of our shirts and attracted thousands of mosquitoes and black flies. We tore leafy branches off low poplar bushes and waved them back and forth across the backs of our necks.

"The road goes all the way up the hill, right to the mine." Dad said. We forged ahead, walking along one wheel track or the other, tall grass growing in between. Occasionally we stopped in a shady spot created by the canopy of maple and birch.

The excursion was like a military expedition. "No stopping to eat raspberries until the way back."

I don't remember carrying water bottles or bug spray. The one-kilometre walk seemed endless but the drudgery was forgotten when we reached the opening of a huge, gravel strewn clearing. Past the red and white sign that read ' "Danger, Keep Out," ' we discovered a fifty-metre long building constructed with rusted metal sheeting. "That was the cookhouse and barracks for the miners," Dad said. "That big stone fireplace and chimney over to the left is where they smelted the lead."

We later learned the Frontenac Draper Lake Mine had a long history starting in 1866 when unknown miners sank the first shaft to 24 metres and extracted 2000 tons of ore by 1870. In 1875 the Frontenac Lead Mining and Smelting Company excavated the same shaft to a depth of 81 metres, excavating another 2000 tons of ore. Other companies followed, sinking two more shafts, constructing a mill at the first shaft, then blasting two more shafts. The Kingston Smelting Company, operated by the India Lake Lead Mining Company produced 38,527 pounds of lead from the 2,500 tons of ore mined over the final four years of mine activity. As late as 1958, developers still sampled ore in hopes of finding valuable minerals.

We each carried a six-quart basket Mom had left over from when she bought peaches. As we inspected the rocks, Dad explained what to look for. "Those speckled rocks are granite.

Just like our swimming rock. It's a solid base for the lead, just like our swimming rock is for our family."

Each year we discovered more of the good lead samples had been picked over by other treasure seekers coming in from the road away from the lake.

"Stay clear of the pits. There's water about thirty feet below the surface and who knows how deep it is. If you fall in we'll never see you again. And, don't pick up anything that looks like dynamite." We had no idea what dynamite looked like so avoided anything suspicious.

Dad trusted our good sense. Keeping the holes at a safe distance still gave us lots of territory to explore. We coveted lumps of clean white quartz and cylindrical granite core samples. Soon the baskets brimmed with treasures. Fools gold, iron pyrites, glittered in the sun. We stuffed extras in our jeans pockets. Despite the slight slope of the trek back to the lake the weighty treasures dragged us down.

"Everybody carry their own basket."

We never dreamed of asking Dad to carry for us. He expected us to be responsible for our own baskets. Pleased with our precious finds, and proud of the ability to carry a full basket, we hobbled along. Visions of jumping in the lake from the Front Rock, cool lake water cleansing the sweat from our weary backs the minute we got back to the island, kept us going. The effort was worth it. We loved the sparkle of the iron pyrites and weight of the lead pieces.

When we did venture away from the lake, it counted as a major event worthy of planning and preparation. Off island, Mom returned to her 50s housewife identity. She abandoned her shorts and halter in favour of a more formal feminine sundress. Dad wore long pants and a shirt with a collar. We rifled our dresser drawers for clean shorts and T-shirts.

Every year, somewhere near the end of Dad's holidays, we followed the winding dirt road to Chaffeys' Locks. Just as hot

This way to the Opinicon Lodge and Chaffey's Locks 2021. —Barry Hodgins

dogs taste best roasted on a stick over an open campfire, as hot chocolate warms the heart more after tobogganing on a crisp winter day, the picnic lunches Mom packed for us went down best at Chaffey's Lock.

Sensing an outing, Roger stood, tail wagging, in the rowboat.

"Everyone have hats and a sweater?" Mom tucked the picnic basket in the shade of the front peak.

"Everyone have a last shot at the pot?" Dad said, jiggling the metal pegs of the oars into the oarlocks. Leaving behind tall bulrushes interspersed with purple pickerel weed, we slid through the white lotus-like blossoms of the water lilies. Dad aimed the bow toward the farmhouse shore and a day of adventure.

Roger assumed his customary figurehead position, nostrils flared for unfamiliar scents. A faint breeze rippled his blond and white fur. Dad rowed, his back to the heat of the morning rays. Mom and I sat opposite facing him in the middle seat. Doug and Donna positioned themselves on either side in the stern, each armed with a personal canoe paddle carved by Grandpa.

"Dip! Dad called, to synchronize their paddle strokes. "Dip!"

Their paddles entered the water in unison with the oar blades. The boat surged forward, aided slightly by prevailing winds.

The 23 km drive from Draper Lake to our outing destination of Chaffey's Lock led us over a hilly, winding dirt road and constituted another great adventure in itself. After what seemed like forever we descended a steep hill, lined by huge maples and tiny cottages, then crossed a rickety wooden bridge over the narrow waterway at Lock 37 of the Rideau Canal. Farther on, the road swooped in front of the Opinicon Lodge. The stately Victorian lodge loomed grandly on the brow of a green hill surrounded by ancient oaks. Dad pulled into a parking spot close to our favourite picnic table at the lock's edge.

"Put Roger on the leash," Dad said. "Doug, you're in charge. Don't let him run around and bother people."

Mom spread a plastic cloth on the table and doled out the picnic. We set out to ogle the motor launches docked along the edge of the canal where they waited to be admitted into the lock. We watched as staff, led by the lockmaster, cranked the iron mechanisms to operate the lock. Motor launches, signs on their stern indicating ports of call as far away as Toronto, Ottawa or Montreal had been moored overnight waiting for a turn in the lock to continue their journey south.

Attired in crisply ironed tan and green Rideau Canal uniforms, mostly male Queen's University students hired for the summer, the crew waved the boats slowly ahead into the lock.

"Can we go across the gates and watch from the other side?" Doug asked.

"Better wait until the boats are through," Dad said. "You don't want to get caught on the other side and miss lunch."

Mahogany-tanned women in skimpy bikinis, chatting in

French, lolled on boat decks, early cocktails in hand. The lock gates closed behind them. Hairy chested skippers in skimpy speedos and black captain's hats grabbed a long line to tie to the lock wall. The lock gates closed and the valves on the downstream side of the lock began to let the water out of the lock. The boats floated gently down as the water drained. When they reached the level of the next lake, the gates opened and the boaters proceeded south onto Newboro Lake.

Chaffey's, Lock 37 of the Rideau Canal, also known as the Rideau Waterway, is one of forty-seven locks of a 202-km system that connects Canada's capital city of Ottawa to Lake Ontario and the Saint Lawrence River at Kingston. Opened in 1832 as a precaution in case of a war with the United States, it has remained open primarily for pleasure boating. The name Rideau, French for curtain, is derived from the curtain-like appearance of the Rideau River's twin waterfalls where they join the Ottawa River.

John Haggart, a partner in John Sheriff and Company, organized the Chaffey's construction project. Haggart brought in stone from Halladay's quarry, near Elgin, 5 km away during the hot summer of 1828. When most of the crew experienced bouts of malaria, construction slowed. In 1844 a defensible one-storey stone lockmaster's house was built. In 1894 the house was completely renovated and a wood frame back kitchen and second storey added. Curious about the house, we loved snooping around the flower gardens and peeking through the darkly screened front door. Dad told us the current lockmaster, William McIntyre, lived there.

"Don't go peering in the windows," Dad said, "It's a private house. He doesn't need kids hanging around. He's got enough to do keeping the locks going."

After lunch we casually strolled up the sloping lawn toward the Opinicon Lodge, trying our best to look as if we belonged.

"Can we have lunch there sometime?" Donna asked, as we wandered past the flagstone pathway leading to the front door.

Manicured gardens of heart-shaped silver green and variegated hostas interspersed with red geraniums bordered the flat gray rocks, lending an air of opulence. Mom gazed toward the windows of the dining room. Through the multi-paned windows we could see uniformed servers hovering over well-dressed patrons seated at tables with white cloths. It seemed formal and intimidating. We never went inside.

"That's just for the people who rent the lodge cabins. That's where they eat all their meals. Besides, it's too expensive," Mom said.

We were in awe of the Opinicon. With its majestic two-storey, wrap around verandah, dotted with red chairs and potted ferns, it looked like it belonged more on a southern plantation than on the shore of Newboro Lake. In reality, the grand old Opinicon Hotel had slightly more humble beginnings. In 1899 when the first Lockmaster, William Fleming, a private in the 7th Company, Royal Sappers and Miners, retired, he bought the property and built a tourist lodge. Around 1902, William Laishley bought the gorgeous hunk of real estate, added a wing to the building and called it Idylwild. He operated it as a tourist resort until 1904. He sold to a fishing club from Youngstown, Ohio, who operated it as a private club known as the Opinicon Club. Then in 1921 Mae and William Phillips of Pittsburgh purchased it and turned it back into a public tourist resort. It stayed in the hands of the Phillips descendants until it went up for sale in 2014.

In the following years locals and loyal tourists held their collective breath, waiting impatiently, snatching at every rumour regarding the fate of the grand old dame. Was she worth saving? Who could afford to restore her to her former well-earned glory? Chain link fences surrounded the property, mysteriously devoid of signs. Spirits sagged. Finally, the word got out. Fiona McKean and Tobi Lutke of Shopify fame had completed the deal in 2015. They planned to restore and reopen the Opinicon. Excitement reigned when doors opened to grand ceremony in 2017.

"Can we go for ice cream, then?"

Up the road, on the left past the lodge, we reached a small frame building, the Opinicon General Store. We ignored the peeling pale salmon-coloured paint. Doug stayed outside with Roger. We followed Dad through the dark green screen door into the cool interior. On that hot, humid and hazy Ontario summer afternoon the Opinicon ice cream parlour felt like heaven. Four tall chrome stools covered in mint green Naugahyde stood in front of a shiny silver countertop. As we entered, a young girl in a crisp white uniform and cap grabbed a silver ice cream scoop from a jar of murky water.

"May I help you?" She leaned forward over a freezer full of choices. We strained ahead for a good view. The front row showed the usual chocolate, vanilla and strawberry, alongside Mom and Dad's favourite, butterscotch pecan. In the second row I spied my choice, rainbow sherbet. Donna picked the more exotic burgundy cherry and Doug opted for chocolate. Roger didn't seem to care as long as we saved the last of the cone for him, with some ice cream still in it.

Fingers sticky from dripping ice cream, we retraced our steps to the parking lot. "Let Roger finish your cones before you get in the car. Don't want him slobbering all over the seats," Dad said, as he put the key in the lock. "Then, go wash off your hands in the canal. Mom's got a towel."

A perfect day. No errands, no set timeline, no discussion of the debated cost of foot frontage to buy back the island. Near the end of his holidays Dad relaxed into the spirit of a low-key family outing.

CHAPTER 22
OTTAWA OR BUST

Late August 2019

*D*oug pulls his boat up to the dock at Turkey Island. His *daughter Drue pads barefoot down the path from her cottage. The second her toes touch the dock, he speaks.* "Our offer was accepted for the lead mine property. Let's call Kerry."

With that deal Doug, his two daughters Kerry Shales Brooker and Drue Shales Pollenz and their respective spouses Barry Brooker and Gary Pollenz, preserve about three-hundred metres of water access only shoreline, preventing future development that could have changed the lake forever. The property on the lakeside of the lead mine, the location of our campfire with Jamie on the far shore, is now protected as part of the Shales compound. As yet an unclaimed stage for expanded family. Room to grow with space on all sides.

July 2002. Ottawa or Bust
"Do you see them?"

I straighten up in my kayak as we approach Chaffey's Lock for a look under the bridge.

"There they are. Right on time." Barry leans forward in his red Prospector canoe and points to Doug's Honda Odyssey van. It crosses the bridge with a rumble. Dad and Doug's wife Margo wave.

Barry and I are on the first day of our 200 km camping and paddling trip from Kingston Mills to Ottawa on the Rideau Canal. Early that morning we put our canoe and kayak in the water at Kingston Mills, 28 kilometres from Draper Lake. We've spent the last week drying slices of kiwi and fresh strawberries to add to our oatmeal porridge for breakfasts and packing kamut pasta and dried soups for dinners. Crackers, cheese, trail mix and chocolate work well for lunches.

Doug, Margo and Dad have arrived from the lake with a picnic lunch. As usual, Margo spreads a cloth over the picnic table on the lawn beside the canal. The fresh egg salad sandwiches and brownies she prepared taste even better after our morning of paddling from Kingston Mills. The faraway look in Dad's eyes tells me he's not the only one missing Mom and thinking of past picnics here at Chaffey's. He looks up from his reverie.

"Anyone have room left for ice cream? It's on me."

The screen door of the ice cream parlour slams behind us as we wander back to a small slip where we docked the canoe and kayak.

Cones finished, we board our boats for the afternoon paddle to Upper Brewers Lock, our first overnight camping spot. "Tenting tonight, tenting tonight." Dad sings me a few lines of his favourite camp song as he pushes my kayak and Barry's canoe off from the shore. He is still humming as he heads back to the van. I'm dreaming of trips up the Nile.

CHAPTER 23
THE SEARCH FOR THE PERFECT BARN BRUSH

August 1955

"I stubbed my toe. It's bleeding!" I plopped myself down on the Front Rock and inspected the damage. "The rock's always too slippery." Head down I muttered to myself.

"Third time this week," Mom said. "It's just a scrape. Stick your toe in the water. That'll stop the bleeding."

I pouted. I considered her response lacking in sympathy. Nothing but practical instruction from a no-nonsense trained nurse.

"And, whose turn was it to brush the rock?" Mom said.

I lifted my damaged toe out of the water and peered down to examine it further. I avoided Mom's glare.

Dad looked up from his book. "I guess it's time for a new brush. That old barn brush Elwood gave us has hardly any bristles left. Tomorrow's soon enough."

It was to be a day built around errands. Mom assembled a substantial picnic first thing. "You never know how long we'll be away," she said.

We started early the next morning, all five of us. Mist covered the lake, blanketing our shoulders as the rowboat approached the mainland. The closest source of a new barn brush was Charlie Hughson's general store. It stood at the corners, Perth Road Village. Dreams of ice cream, soda pop, Dell comics like *Archie* and *Little Lulu* and Classics Comics like *Prisoner of Zenda* had kept me awake the night before. How much allowance had I saved? What could I get with my weekly allowance of 25 cents?

Mom and Dad rarely wavered from our stipulated weekly allowance. "We're training you to plan ahead and spend your money wisely."

Math and budgeting rapidly gained importance. Mom and Dad left final decisions to each of us. Regular Dell comics, a freshly scooped ice cream cone and Orange Crush each cost 10 cents. Classic comics cost 15 cents. Sacrifices had to be made. But which? The short drive barely allowed enough time to ponder a final verdict before we arrived at Charlie Hughson's store. Serious choices loomed before us.

Purchases completed, the three of us sat side by side on the edge of the cement steps in front of the store. Some days ice cream dripped down our sticky fingers. Other times the chilly condensation of an Orange Crush bottle cooled our sunburned cheeks. We went outside to wait for Mom and Dad. Heads down we devoured the latest issue of *Little Lulu*. I held it. Lulu was my favourite. Doug and Donna leaned in on either side. Dad lingered by the counter to catch up on local gossip with Charlie.

"Any idea of a good place to buy a strong, stiff-bristled barn brush?"

Charlie hesitated and then, in a low mumble recommended his competition. "You could try Scullions."

Meanwhile, Roger assumed his usual position below us as we sat on the cement step in front of the store. When we licked our cones, Roger salivated, ogling the last inch of each cone he knew would be reserved for him. His pink tongue lolled out the side of his mouth from heat and anticipation. His brown eyes flickered ravenously from one of us to the others, checking our progress.

Trousdale's General Store, Sydenham, Ontario 2021. —Barry Hodgins

The last of the cones demolished we all trooped across the street after Dad. Mr. Scullion was clean out of barn brushes.

When Dad couldn't find basic hardware equipment at Hughson's, we'd usually make the fifteen-minute drive southwest on Highway 10 to the village of Sydenham. This time Dad combined the errand with a family history tour. "Let's drive by the house where my mother, your Grandma Shales was born."

Born Eva Spray Boyce, Grandma grew up on Brewery Street. The Boyces, staunch teetotalers, thought their street name totally inappropriate, a tad scandalous. Grandpa often regaled us with tales of driving away with his new bride Spray from their afternoon wedding in the Boyce's parlour. They sat tall and proud in the first horseless carriage used in early 1900s Sydenham to transport a bride and groom, in their case, two newly minted teachers, away on their honeymoon.

Trousdale's hardware store stood in the heart of the village at the intersection of three roads. A warren of hardware wonders, the Trousdale family emporium crammed every inch of space, floor to rafters with myriad farming, fishing and homemaking implements. Some looked as if they had been there, gathering dust, since Trousdale's Hardware opened in 1836. While Dad continued his hunt for a barn brush, I was on the lookout for a new bamboo fishing pole. Dad walked me over to the long mahogany counter. Mom, Doug and Donna trailed behind.

"I'm looking for a barn brush. Patti, here, is looking for a new fishing pole." Dad smiled at the kindly-looking woman behind the ancient cash register. Mrs. Trousdale stopped rolling the brown packaging paper off the roll, smoothed her apron around her hips and looked up at us.

"Sorry. Out of brushes." Then turning to me she said,

"Just wait a minute. Nobe must be around here somewhere. I'm sure he can find something for you," she said. "Nobe," she shouted down the length of the store. Mr. Trousdale appeared, his sparse white hair more rumpled than his greying overalls.

"Go with Mr. Trousdale," Dad said. "I'm going to buy some nails while we're here."

Alone and a bit nervous, although I'm not sure why, I dragged myself behind the shuffling footsteps of the curmudgeonly but benign Noble Trousdale. I followed up and down several levels of the store, sections created by haphazard additions over the years. In search of my bamboo pole, we squeezed through narrow passageways fashioned by furniture and appliances precariously piled on either side. It was said that Nobe, as he was known to locals, had an extensive memory of the store's inventory in his head and if he didn't have what a customer wanted, he could get it by Tuesday. Finally, puffing from exertion and dust, he stretched his right arm into a corner. Wedged behind a stack of tall black rubber boots and army green hip waders stood a ten-foot-long bamboo pole. "Don't have too much call for these," he said, handing it to me. "Carry it straight up so you don't poke somebody in the eye."

With that he turned his attention to readjusting a tower of galvanized pails snaking perilously toward the ceiling.

The family reconvened on the sidewalk.

"That's one thing down. But we're still out of luck with the barn brush. Trousdale said Vandervoort's on Princess Street might have one. We're out now. May as well go into Kingston," Dad said.

Forty minutes later we were parked in Kingston, a city of almost three-hundred thousand. For a brief period, from 1841 to 1844, Kingston boasted status as the first capital of what was then the United Provinces of Canada.

Our stroll along Princess Street in downtown Kingston past the grand two-storey limestone storefronts felt important, a bit surreal, like a visit into history. Vanderwoort's original structure, built in 1817, had previously served as an inn, a library, a ballroom, a military hospital and a grammar school. Since 1890, 77 Princess Street has been a hardware store, first operated by the Elliot Brothers. In 1947 the Vanderwoort cousins, Claude and Dean, took over the business.

We filed in after mom and Dad. We loved the creaky, slanting wooden floors, exposed limestone walls and triangular bins of nails. Dad asked at the front counter. "Looks like Vanderwort's is all out, too." We followed Dad out to the sidewalk and turned left. "We could try down at the bottom of Princess. S and R," Mom said.

The thought of a trip to S and R always revved us up. We couldn't wait to explore all four storeys of weird, wonderful, often unconventional items. Located at 27 Princess Street, the limestone monolith overlooked Lake Ontario. The 1812 building once served as a home and a store called Commercial Mart. George Browne, the architect responsible for Kingston's iconic dome-crowned City Hall, designed the dominating commercial structure in 1812.

After many years of commercial use, the building became the Wormwith Piano Factory, then morphed into office and warehouse space. In 1959, Percy Robinson and his brother-in-law Morrie Smith, who had formerly operated Berlin's, a menswear store on King Street, purchased the building and opened S and R.

The best part of S and R was the elevator. And, its operator. No one was allowed in the elevator until he offered a formal invitation. "Step right to the back of the car, please. Step right back." Stone faced, dark hair protruding from his cap, the uniformed operator straightened his posture, swung shut the squeaky see-through iron gate and pulled the lever. "Going up."

Gaze unwavering, he never cracked a smile as he announced the wares of each floor as the car ascended. "Hardware, women's clothing, shoes, menswear."

Rumour has it he was sacked for making rude, inappropriate comments to customers. Maybe that was the origin of our family saying, "Ladies lingerie (or sometimes the even more scandalous ladies' underwear) going down." No one could remember if they heard this at Eaton's or S and R. Doug and Donna relentlessly thought it hilarious to call this out when they sank the raft in the deep water off the Front Rock. Roger and I were invariably left frantically treading water.

Barn brush found and paid for, back out on the street Dad slung the brush over his shoulder. Decked out in clean trousers, a collared shirt no longer quite fresh enough for his downtown Toronto office job and polished shoes, Dad looked like a city slicker. With a barn brush casually slung over his shoulder he caused the occasional double take from passers-by.

Downtown errand complete, we piled into the car for the grand finale of the day, a supper picnic on the grounds of Old Fort Henry.

I shivered with anticipation at the thought of the route ahead. From downtown Kingston Highway 2 continued across the LaSalle Causeway. Built in 1917 the causeway replaced the

1829 Penny Bridge, a wooden toll bridge with a swing section to allow passage of marine vessels. The first permanent crossing had been a cable ferry built in 1786.

The current version featured a lift bridge between two fixed sections. Too nervous to enjoy the view of the Cataraqui River on one side and the beginning of the Rideau Canal on the other, my shoulders stiffened. No matter how many times we crossed, I imagined our car careening off the edge of the bridge and plunging into the river just as the bridge lifted. "What if the bridge lifts when we're on it?" No one else in the car spoke.

"The man in the booth will see us coming. Don't worry," Dad said. "I'll honk to remind him before we start over the lift section." We approached the booth at a snail's pace. Dad honked. Both men nodded. I closed my eyes and held my breath. One, two, three, four, five. We reached the other side unscathed.

Past the gates of the Royal Military College, up the hill, the car clattered over the dry moat wooden bridge separating the advanced battery, the front grouping of guns, from the main fort, then stopped. A young uniformed member of the Fort Henry Guard snapped to attention, saluted and leaned in toward Dad's open window. "Good afternoon, sir. Welcome to Old Fort Henry. Are you planning to take a tour of the fort?"

"Are you planning to take a tour of the fort?" Donna and I mimicked in unison whispers from the back seat. A Queen's University student, on his summer job, he valiantly attempted to appear official. Giggles barely stifled, Donna and I slumped down in the back seat.

"Maybe later." Dad invariably implied a tour of the fort was imminent in order to secure a premium parking space inside the fortress. We knew the tour wouldn't happen. "Not in the budget," Dad would say.

Out of the car and outside the fort wall, with Roger on his leash we faced a cool breeze from Lake Ontario. We rounded the corner and settled at a picnic table overlooking downtown

Kingston. We eagerly devoured the usual egg salad sandwiches, carrots, and celery stick boats with cheddar cheese.

Dad pointed downtown. "Look at that. You can see the spires of Kingston."

Back inside the fortress we crossed the cobbled parade ground, entered the souvenir shop and ordered ice cream cones. We licked. Roger salivated. No electricity on the island meant no refrigerator, no freezer, no ice cream. We never said no.

On the days Fort Henry didn't appear on the agenda, Wilmot's Dairy on Bath Road, got penciled in. The traffic circle at the intersection of Bath Road and Princess Street seemed an insolvable puzzle, making ice cream synonymous with, as far as I was concerned, hazardous driving situations. "How do you know there won't be any other cars in the circle?" Again I was ignored, the worrier in the crowd.

I shut my eyes against any rapidly approaching traffic. Once inside Wilmot's cool, air-conditioned interior, peering through condensation at the extensive array of ice cream flavours, I always knew the risk was worth it.

As exhilarating as it was to be away from the island, a marathon day in the smothering mainland heat exhausted us all. By the time we docked at the island the sky glowed like a ripe summer peach.

"Can we go for a night swim?" we chorused. Mom agreed, happy to lead the way.

We changed into our bathing suits, ran across the lawn and stepped carefully down the still slippery rock. One by one we plunged into the rejuvenating water, then turned on our backs to float and search for shooting stars.

Dad handed me my towel as we walked together across the lawn to the cottage. "Your turn to brush tomorrow morning, Patti."

CHAPTER 24
GOING TO TOWN

August 2021

*G*rateful indoor dining has resumed in Ontario, I slide into the banquette and remove my Covid-19 mask. We've been wearing medical face masks indoors since mid-March 2020. I wonder when it will end and if we will ever be able to travel internationally again. I know we're lucky to have access to protective vaccinations. Not everyone in the world is so fortunate. I worry about our friends in Nepal, particularly the children in Ratmate village where I was a volunteer teacher and those in Aprik village where our non-profit Nepal One Day at a Time built a school.

"I'll have a glass of the Kim Crawford sauvignon blanc, please. Six ounce is fine."

It is, after all, only 3 p.m.

"Clamato juice, spelled with a C," Barry says. "And, no ice, please."

Silently I thank my lucky stars for the air conditioning and my self-appointed, permanent designated driver. We're more than ready to relax into a late lunch at Milestones Grill and Bar at the bottom of Princess Street in Kingston. We love Milestones. The first one opened in 1989 on Vancouver's Denman Street in Vancouver. The young, hip clientele enjoyed the casual menu and expansive views over English Bay. We frequented it often, especially during my five-year stint as principal of Lord Roberts Elementary, three blocks away in the heart of Vancouver's West End.

In Kingston, when S and R closed its doors in 2009, locals

wondered what would become of the grand old edifice that housed the multi-level department store. Two years later, after extensive renovations, the limestone structure reinvented itself into trendy office space, grounded by a Milestones restaurant on the main floor. While Kingston's location lacks the views offered by its West Coast counterpart, the Princess Street spot more than makes up for this oversight with its historical significance and architectural charm. Exposed limestone walls, ridiculously high ceilings and the original arched windows preserved the dignity and individual character. I adore the Victorian limestone facades of Kingston buildings. And, I also love late lunches at Milestones. So since it opened its doors in 2011 it has become one of our regular haunts, providing a taste of Vancouver in our chosen summer neighbourhood.

Every second Thursday is laundry day. It's already been a long day. We loaded the boat with duffels of dirty laundry and the cooler bag filled with empty grocery bags. I gave the final push away from our island dock at about 8 am. Out of habit I start early, the way Donna and I used to. We always planned to get back to the lake in time for a swim before dinner. Barry directed from the stern seat while I rowed across to our mainland parking lot in Grandpa's seven decades old red rowboat. We loaded the car and headed south on Highway 10 from the end of Shales Road.

Long gone is our original tradition of metal laundry tubs, washboards and swirling sheets in the lake. More environmentally conscious these days, a new routine exists, established first by Mom, continued by Donna and me, and now, by me alone.

Laundry days make me feel sad. It was on one of these days I first noticed early signs of dementia in Donna. It was a small thing. She was usually a decisive person. I knew something was wrong when she spent more time than usual examining each piece of laundry, not able to easily decide which needed to be done in hot or cold water. She was only sixty-nine.

To preserve our pristine lake, I do laundry off island at Frontenac Mall Coin Laundry on Bath Road in Kingston. The owner, Fernando, greets me when Barry drops me off, along with several bags of dirty clothes, sheets and towels, at 9 am. His laundromat family tradition is as long as our own. Fernando took over the business from his cousin Tony a few years ago. The machines are a bit dented and at least a few are always out of order, but Fernando is always there with a smile.

"Missed you last summer," he says. "It must have been hard not to come to the cottage."

"It was. Horrible. Missed you, too. We drove this year. First time since 2013. Still afraid to get on a plane. Covid-19 certainly put the kibosh on travel plans for so many people."

I hand him a twenty. He counts out the requisite number of Toonies, Loonies and quarters I'll need for the washers and dryers. Washers loaded, I walk into the mall. Pleased to find the Chit Chat Café still going strong despite long Covid closures, I order the all-day breakfast with a coffee and sit at my favourite table. Every step of the morning routine, the row, the drive to Kingston, the idiosyncrasies of individual laundromat machines and now our favourite café breakfast order, is filled with memories. Faded ones of Mom, mostly of Donna. I pick up a book for company with my eggs over easy.

Two hours later Barry arrives to rescue me with my bags of carefully folded clean laundry. He's been busy. One of us always seems to have a physio appointment, the result of ski injuries or shoulder issues from swimming and paddling. Today is his turn. With the remaining time I sent him on a mission to find a new barn brush. The Front Rock is getting slippery and the bristles on Dad's old brush are worn down, almost useless. Doug, Donna and I have replaced it several times since. It's my turn this year.

"Did you find it?" I ask, as we schlep the bags into the back of the car.

"Yep. At the Depot. Good stiff bristles. Should work well," Barry says.

"Leave the cooler bag out. Let's get groceries, then have a late lunch, so we can relax. Milestones?"

"Sounds good to me," he says, turning the wheel towards downtown Kingston.

Our server returns with the drinks. We order the usual, California Spring Salad with grilled salmon. There's comfort in the familiar when the quality is there. By 4 p.m. we're back on Hwy 10, travelling north.

As we near Perth Road Village memories of eating ice cream on the step of Charlie Hughson's store with Roger looking on dance into my head. I mention this to Barry. He takes the next left turn.

"Where are you going?"

"Sydenham. Trousdale's," he says.

"Excellent idea."

The screen door of Trousdale's General store, still touted as Canada's oldest general store, slaps behind us. I swear it's the same door I went through that day to buy my fishing pole. The door may be the same but Ginny Trousdale has transformed the premises. Hardware can now be found at her husband John's Home Hardware on the edge of the village. The original store, now a charming emporium of vintage-inspired cottage games, kitchenware, trendy apothecary items, upscale summer clothing ensembles, most importantly serves fresh scooped ice cream. I climb the stairs to the back room where Nobe found my fishing pole to view an assortment of faux barn board signs and décor items favoured by today's cottagers.

My Covid-19 mask prevents me from licking my rapidly melting espresso flake cone, so I walk past the table of nature puzzles and fabric-lined baskets to the door. Refreshed and replete I'm ready for the row home.

CHAPTER 25
THE NEED FOR SPEED

1955

Just after breakfast I heard the high whine of a motor. We looked up from the lawn to glimpse Uncle Jack roaring around the end of our island. He sat tall in the stern of his plywood speedboat, hand on the tiller of a 7 horsepower Johnson outboard, the most powerful motor we had ever seen. Catching frogs for fishing bait would have to wait. The impressive craft barreled toward us, the high bow catching the breeze. The stern exhibited dangerously minimal freeboard due to Great Uncle Jack's considerable bulk. Grandpa's elder brother, also born and raised in the farmhouse on the mainland, and his wife, Great Aunt Laura, summered at their glorious two-storey cottage on the island behind ours.

Donna, Doug and I practically collided on the dock, vying for the privilege of catching Uncle Jack's bow rope.

"Anyone want to come for a ride?"

Uncle Jack stood, right hand leaning on the white hood of the Johnson. My dad had many wonderful talents. Solid dock construction wasn't one of them. He preferred narrow catwalks with more than a hint of a bounce. With three of us on the dock already, we knew it couldn't take any more weight. Before Uncle Jack had a chance to step out of the boat, we clambered in. I popped into the front seat, fingers firmly entwined in the bow rope. Doug and Donna shared the middle seat. Doug faced backward, watching Uncle Jack's every move. Dad stepped onto the dock and pushed us off toward the drop off. Mom waved.

No doubt looking forward to a quiet cup of coffee.

"Heads down." Donna and Doug leaned forward out of harm's way. Uncle Jack pulled the cord, his elbow shooting back up and over Doug's head. The engine rumbled, Uncle Jack switched the gear to reverse and backed the craft smoothly past the weedy drop off into the deep water. Doug's eyes were glued to Uncle Jack's hands as he switched into forward gear and revved the engine. We surged forward like a loon taking flight, hydroplaning the surface at a speed beyond previous experience or imagination. Uncle Jack steered the skiff once around the entire island, then performed a sail past dangerously close to the Front Rock. Strands of frizzy curls whipped my cheeks. For one brief moment I dared to take one hand off the bow rope to wave furiously at Mom and Dad. Moments later we rounded the tip of our island for the second time. Uncle Jack throttled down then slid the sleek craft gracefully alongside the low, square dock at his island.

I tossed the bow rope to Aunt Laura, who stood grinning on the shady dock. Her long white hair was fashioned in a messy bun, well before Meaghan Markle made the style popular in 2019. Wispy tendrils framed her milky indoor artist's complexion, lightly draping the shoulders of her billowy ensemble. No sandals with ankle socks for her. To us, Uncle Jack and Aunt Laura exuded instant charisma. Habitually involved in some project or other, general cottage maintenance for Uncle Jack or more artistic endeavours for Aunt Laura, both often sported paint under their fingernails.

Uncle Jack unsuccessfully disguised his portly frame with cottage cast offs. Beige cotton pants, dotted with a collage of boat and cottage paint, hitched up with a belt fashioned from the same rope used for the bowline on his boat. A threadbare sleeveless undershirt stretched over his barrel chest.

Many years later, during a visit to his home in Florida, I saw his retirement photo. It was almost impossible to reconcile the Uncle Jack I knew at the cottage with the distinguished gentleman in the photo, slicked down hair, wearing a white dinner jacket. Like Grandpa and Uncle Walter, Dr. John Shales, aka our adored Uncle Jack, graduated from Queen's University, completed both a Masters and PhD and moved to Indiana. He became an esteemed tenured professor of education. Ball State University in Muncie named a building for him, Shales Hall. To us, he remained a fun guy, always game for an adventure.

Aunt Laura led the way up the rocky path to their cottage. We rubbed our bare feet on the ragged mat then padded onto the flagstones of the spacious screened-in sleeping porch wrapping three sides of the building. An aging pump organ featuring several rows of keys and mysterious looking knobs stood against the interior wall of the cottage.

"Can I play the organ?" Donna asked.

Donna and Doug had had a few years of piano lessons, but there was more to playing Aunt Laura's organ than knowing the keys.

"Sit beside me, here." Aunt Laura patted the water-stained bench in invitation. She showed Donna which stops to pull out for different sound effects. Then she demonstrated how to pump the pedals back and forth to create enough air to produce sound from the ancient instrument. "Okay. You give it a try."

Donna slid forward on the bench. Her feet barely stretched to the pedals. Aunt Laura's feet slid beside Donna's. Feet and fingers mobilized in unison, they played chopsticks and one verse of "Country Gardens". Legs far too short to reach the pedals, I watched for a bit, then listened while Doug peppered Uncle Jack with questions about the seven horsepower boat engine.

Once past the porch, inside the main cottage, we stood for a moment in silent awe in front of the towering stone fireplace. We gazed up at the winding stairway leading to the second-floor loft. An artist as well as a musician, Aunt Laura had woven her magic into a huge white string spider web caught between the rails of the upstairs mezzanine.

The grand old cottage, a vessel overflowing with memories and traditions, narrowly missed total destruction one late August weekday in 2010. We didn't yet know the new owners very well. Distant relatives of Aunt Laura, they returned to their nearby farm on a Sunday evening after a relaxing cottage weekend. Sadly, they had failed to thoroughly douse their Saturday evening campfire. Five days later I smelled smoke coming toward our island. Curious and concerned, Barry and I jumped into the canoe and circled the densely treed island.

"The smoke isn't coming from the fireplace."

My memory fixed the origin of the smoke as somewhere in the centre of the island, well away from the stone fireplace. "There's no boat at the dock. It looks like nobody's there. We'd better check."

We paddled over, stroking furiously against the wind, then tied the canoe and started up the familiar path, calling out hello. When no one answered, we continued up to the cottage. What we found frightened us. Ashes smoldered in the fire pit. A cloud of heat and fumes led halfway across the island to the base of a towering White Pine. Orange flames licked its roots. Only a few wisps of smoke were visible above the pines.

The five-minute paddle back to our dock seemed to take forever. Barry grabbed a maddock and shovel and returned to the fire. Cell phones still didn't work on our island. I used the landline to alert the local fire department and close neigbours. A stalwart crew of cottagers converged on the dock, formed a bucket brigade up the path to the building, scurrying as quickly as a gaggle of retired cottagers could muster. None of them had noticed the smoke.

Barry and local artist Jamie Brick, descendant of Clarence Stoness who sold Grandpa Shales our island, dug a trench. They uncovered fiery embers that had travelled along the roots deep beneath the surface of the earth from the fire pit to the tall pine. Jamie and Barry decided the situation merited breaking the lock on the cottage door to turn on the electric pump. Once the pump was switched on, pressure built, activating the hose lying at the side door.

Emergency somewhat under control, I took a break from bucket duty and ventured inside for a bit of nostalgia. It was at least fifty years since I had set foot in the cottage. It was as if no time had passed. Memories flooded my being. Despite the pumping adrenalin of the emergency situation, I hesitated, standing still, temporarily lost in time. Everything looked the same. I half expected to find Uncle Jack leaning on the stone mantle of the fireplace, hear the wheezy tones of the pump organ or find Aunt Laura peering over the railing of the mezzanine behind her intricately woven web. The noise of the action outside snapped me back to the present. Strings grayed by time, the spider's lair still hung, miraculously intact.

Within the hour the Perth Road Village volunteer firefighters arrived on the scene, relieving the weary bucket bearing retirees. Led by Cousin Mary's husband, fire captain Wayne Newport, brigade members immersed a powerful water pump in the lake and unfurled their modern industrial hose to the fire site. Swiping soot from our sweaty faces, our crew stood back exhausted while the local volunteer firefighters finished the job.

My dread of the possibility of island fires had alerted me early to investigate the source of the smoke. My memory of the position of the cottage on the island alerted my curiosity and the ingenuity and support of community saved the day.

One week later Wayne might have had his ski boat out of the lake for winter storage. There would have been no easy way to take the pump to the island. Sometimes a fast motor is a blessing.

In the early years, motors of any kind fascinated us. Johnson and Evinrude were household names. That first two-horse engine bequeathed by Uncle Orie provided early training. A relic of the early 40s, it featured an open flywheel that spun at the top of the motor when running. To start it, one had to wind a rope, knotted at one end to attach to the flywheel, which had several slots at the outside edge. The other end of the rope had a small wooden toggle to grab for a quick yank. Doug often took several tries to start it. I loved to sit beside him in the stern seat.

"Don't put your fingers near the top of the motor." He didn't need to remind me. The idea of my fingers getting caught in the flywheel scared me enough to keep my hands in my lap.

According to Doug, that motor died after a year. Dad replaced it with another secondhand version. No speed control. On and off switch only. It's a wonder we have all our fingers. But those eggbeaters got us where we wanted to go, most often to our favourite fishing spots.

With Dad's permission we chopped and trimmed small cedars to make anchor poles. We drove the stakes into the soft marl bottom of various sandbars and weedy drop-off locations visible from the ront rock. Depending on the wind and time of day we tied up to the poles, keeping the boat in one place so all three of us could fish at once. No nibbles in one spot? No problem. Donna untethered us from the stake, Doug wound the motor and gave it a pull. We trolled our lines to the next location.

Those motors were light, easy enough for Doug to haul over the short portage to go fishing in a nearby, uninhabited lake. On Sunday mornings, the turnover day for the farm cottage renters, we were allowed to use Uncle Elwood's red wooden rowboat, left briefly unused on the shore of Spectacle Lake, at the end of the portage trail. No need to portage a canoe. The well-trodden portage, established by our ancestors before the turn of the century, remained a family favourite.

By my ninth summer our family had graduated to a series of secondhand five or six horsepower Johnson motors, often hand-me-downs from Grandpa. Those outboards featured shiny white hoods to protect our fingers. Even running at their highest speed the stalwart motors barely pushed our cumbersome rowboat at a rate slightly faster than rowing. Still, with a forward and reverse gear, and a low speed perfect for trolling the weedy drop-offs, we forged ahead into the modern age.

Small motors were perfect for us. They kept us busy. We loved running errands for ice, bread, vegetables and berries. And, after swimming, fishing constituted our main source of entertainment. We were in heaven. Mom even got a few minutes once in a while to sit in a lounge chair, put her feet up, sip tea and read while we were gone.

CHAPTER 26

ROWING AWAY FROM CLIMATE CHANGE

July 1995

*I*n my early thirties I emigrated to the West Coast, met and married an adventurous guy. With Barry by my side, I learned to maneuver whitewater rivers in a canoe and kayak, navigate a sailboat along the Pacific coast and hike the mountain trails of British Columbia. Back at the lake, things were evolving. Some shoreline lots changed hands. Newcomers refurbished old cottages or built new ones and a few opted for permanent lakeside homes. Fleets of 14-foot aluminum boats powered by 10 HP engines buzzed around the islands. A couple of Sea-doos disturbed the serenity briefly, but sensing they didn't belong, skulked off on their trailers to friendlier waters. Residents boiled or filtered lake water, no longer deemed safe to drink. Underwater cables carried electricity to the islands.

During a visit with my parents in 1996 Barry noticed a dramatic difference in my mood and sense of wellbeing the minute my bare feet touched island soil. My shoulders relaxed and smile widened after a swim off the Front Rock. As ever, the lake fulfilled my summer soul. Mom and Dad offered us a spot to build our own bunkie on the back of the island at Third Rock. We immediately accepted. Two years of sketching and discussing, followed by planning, permits and board of variance pleas followed. Blueprints completed, supplies ordered, we were ready to start construction.

The lumber company delivered materials to the family parking lot. That part was easy. DIY island construction demanded family co-ordination and collaboration. Moving lumber and supplies to the building site consumed the first few days. Like a barn-raising bee of the past, all family boat owners volunteered for service. Siblings, spouses, cousins and in-laws carried lumber down the path, loaded their boats, motored to our construction site, unloaded and stacked lumber, then went back and did it all over again. Barry led the parade with Dad's borrowed tin boat and motor.

On July 14, 1995, corner posts and strings finally set out to delineate our single room bunkie foundation, we retired to our tent. That's when we heard, sometime after midnight on Bastille Day, what sounded like a massive locomotive approaching at fearsome speed. Seconds later the force of a 200 kph wind, combined with a torrential downpour, caused our tent to implode leaving us in a tangle of broken poles and drenched nylon. Trees crashed inches from our elbows. Metres away at the building site, a towering basswood toppled with a thunderous thump, closely paralleling the foundation strings.

Grateful no one was injured, except for my embarrassing case of poison ivy, family and neighbours spent the next few weeks repairing cottages. After eight decades at the lake Dad had never seen a storm like it. Climate change became a hot topic of conversation at morning coffee.

Shell of the bunkie complete, we returned the boat we had borrowed from Dad and bought a canoe. When Dad died we used his tin boat for a few seasons to transport construction materials to complete the interior of our bunkie. Sad to say, we got used to having it around. Far to often we chose it instead of the canoe or Grandpa's old rowboat for short trips around the lake.

Early one summer, about ten years ago, one brief conversation changed that.

"What's your plan for the day?" I asked Barry at breakfast.

"I think I'll get the aluminum boat in the lake and see if the

motor still runs," Barry said.

"No. Don't. If you get it out, we'll use it instead of rowing or paddling. Let's leave it for this year. We need the exercise and it's better for the environment," I said.

And with that, we decided to leave it flipped over on shore, chained to a tree. The motor remained in the storage shed.

There are still a few motorboats on the lake but most locals travel by kayak, canoe, rowboat or stand up paddleboards. It's as if cottagers simultaneously signed a silent pact to prevent further damage to our beloved retreat.

When I retired in 2005, I bought a double station rowboat, so we could row as a team. When Barrry and I row in tandem, it skims the surface as smoothly as an evening loon. On my own, I prefer my grandfather's rowboat. Boards steamed and curved by a local farmer in the early 40s, its sturdy planks protected by decades of pitch and paint, it transports me to long ago summers when the lake water was drinkable, winds were light and catastrophic storms brought on by global warming, unimaginable.

CHAPTER 27
THE AQUA FLYER
1956

The summer of '56 I turned ten. Donna was fourteen, Doug fifteen. Elvis Presley dominated the radio waves with the raucous sounds of "Don't Be Cruel", Tim Horton still played hockey for the Leafs, and cottage life at Draper Lake just got a whole lot more interesting.

Early one Friday evening in July, a car horn sounded from the mainland, one long, one short, signaling a greatly anticipated arrival. Dad and Doug each had a couple of weeks off from their jobs. Dad, his annual escape from his desk at the Canada Life Assurance Company and Doug, a respite from his first full-time summer job, hauling heavy golf bags at Weston Golf and Country Club where he laboured hot hours as a caddy.

Mom, Jamie, Donna, Donna's best friend Ellen and I gathered on the front lawn. Dressed in shorts and sleeveless tops, our skin glowed pink. My curls frizzed in the moist humid air. Somehow sensing excitement Roger, approaching middle age in dog years, pranced back and forth behind us, tail wagging.

"Have they got it?" I asked.

"I can't see anything yet." Mom raised the binoculars again and focused them toward the shore, left of the farmhouse. "I see a car. It's coming down to the beach by the Cedars Cottage."

"Is there anything behind it? Let me see." Donna almost strangled Mom trying to unleash the binoculars from her neck.

Shoulder to shoulder, we crowded in a row along the edge of the grass, bare toes curled in expectation, eyes squinting against the fiery glare of the deepening sunset.

"There's something behind the car. It looks like a boat." Donna's voice climbed at least a full octave. She and Ellen turned to face each other, clasped hands and started to dance around the lawn, wailing "A wop bop a loo bop a lop bam boom" the opening line of Pat Boone's latest hit "Tutti Frutti". Mom's lips curled. She sent a secret smile in Jamie's direction. Mom and Jamie had taken Donna and Ellen to a Pat Boone concert in Toronto a few months before. Mom considered Pat Boone a more wholesome influence than the unsavoury, hip-swinging newcomer, Elvis Presley.

"I want to look." I reached up to wrestle the binoculars from Donna.

Jamie raised her right hand to shade her brow. "Looks like they got it."

"Hand me the field glasses," Mom said.

"Do you see a big motor? Any water skis?" Donna said.

"Can't tell yet."

We paced nervously, jockeying for possession of the field glasses. On shore we could just make out Dad's silhouette. It looked like he was unhitching a trailer from the car. There was a dark shape on top of it. He dragged the trailer through the soft beach sand into the weedy shallows. A long vessel-shaped object floated out onto the surface of the lake.

"What's happening?" I asked. "Why are they taking so long? Why did they get here so late?"

We thought we could make out Dad and Doug dragging the empty boat trailer back onto the grass above the beach.

"What are they doing?" I asked.

"I think they're rolling up their pants." Binoculars in hand Mom reported they were wading out to the boat-shaped object.

"They climbed in. I think they're on their way."

Moments later, the low throaty rumble of a large outboard motor grumbled across the glassy water. Donna and Ellen danced and sang. The rest of us cheered. Roger wagged his tail.

What seemed an eternity later Dad gingerly maneuvered the four-metre-long Peterborough Aqua Flyer past the tip of our island. As they approached, he and Doug lowered four white rubber fenders. The boat bounced happily off the wooden slats of our rickety dock as if glad to have arrived safely. The low angle of the last rays of sun radiated a rosy glow off the layers of meticulously applied varnish on the narrow cedar strips of the deck. We stared, eyes wide.

Dad's hand rested proprietarily on the white steering wheel. "This black button is the starter. The white handle is to put it into forward and reverse. The red is for emergency stops." There were two rows of seats, with removable slatted backs. It was the most glorious boat we had ever seen on Draper Lake.

Dad's shoulders soon drooped in Friday evening contentment. Right where he loved to be, he was where he felt he belonged, Loon Island - back with his Beach Girl and surrounded by family.

Dad and Doug had had a long day. After work Dad rescued Doug from the golf course, finagled his way through Friday night city traffic, then bumper-to-bumpered all the way to Curry Balmer Marine on Avenue Road in Toronto to pick up the boat and motor. Dad's first time hauling a trailer, the long winding Highway 2 route along Lake Ontario dragged on longer than usual. At ease for now, Dad temporarily erased from his mind the long trip he still had to make on Sunday evening to return the borrowed trailer.

Tanned and fit from lugging leaden bags around golf course greens, Doug couldn't quite manage to disguise his self-satisfied grin. One arm casually draped over the back of the second row seat he hesitated a moment. "Ta-da," he said, as he reached under a blue tarp with a flourish to produce a shiny pair of water skis. He leaned them up against the blue cover of the Evinrude 25 horsepower motor. "I get to go first."

No argument there. He deserved the privilege. His hard-won golf course wages and tips had paid for half the boat and motor.

Donna assumed, because it was the way things usually went

Evening family cruise on the Aqua Flyer with Doug's son Dean at the wheel. —Doug Shales

in our family, she would be next in the water ski lessons pecking order. We didn't even consider Mom and Jamie. After all, Mom turned forty-one that year, and Dad forty. In our view, that made her far too old for waterskiing. And, Jamie must have been well into her 30s.

Donna and I fantasized gliding over the water like Esther Williams in her movies *Million Dollar Mermaid* and *Dangerous When Wet*. Visions of the Cypress Gardens water ski shows every year at the Canadian National Exhibition in Toronto blurred our overblown aspirations. From the splintered wooden bleachers of the Lake Ontario outdoor waterfront theatre we watched our idols while we sat and devoured bags of Tiny Tom's freshly made mini donuts. Lips dusted with icing sugar, we marveled at the two-tiered rows of water skiers. Muscular broad-shouldered men supported shapely women in sparkling costumes, trailing multi-coloured banners. For a family who had never owned a powerful motor, or a ski boat, or had any members who knew how to waterski, we harboured elaborate dreams.

When a few days later a twist of fate altered the expected learn to water ski roster, it was me, not Donna, who learned second, right after Doug. Donna and Ellen turned fourteen that summer. They considered me too juvenile to share in their teenaged pursuits. They preferred gossiping about boys to catching frogs. Afternoons they spread towels on the grass and lay whispering side by side in the sun, basting in baby oil. While flipping glossy magazine pages, they mooned over the marriage of American film star Grace Kelly to Prince Rainier of Monaco. Endless discussions ensued over the latest beauty secrets detailed in *Cosmo*. Smooth, hairlesslegs were *de rigeur*.

"Mom. Ellen's been allowed to shave for months. She brought her razor for me to try. Can I?" Somewhat reluctantly Mom agreed.

That's where the problem began. The next morning Donna and Ellen headed for the Front Rock with Ellen's Gillette Super Speed razor and a towel each. Donna opened a pristine bar of Ivory Soap, chosen for use at the lake because it floated. Ellen unwrapped the white and blue wrapper, dipped the soap in the lake and rubbed her legs vigourously to produce a foamy lather. With the first stroke of the razor along her calf she realized the blade was dull.

"I'm all soapy," Ellen said. "Can you go in my purse and get a fresh razor blade?" Donna found Ellen's bag on the bed in the back room. She reached in, rifled around past the lipstick, hairbrush and Clearasil zit cream, then slid down past the Yardley face powder compact. In those days Gillette sold razor blades in packs of five, in small paper packets. Inside, each blade lay inside an unsealed paper envelope. Donna found a blade all right, but in the jumble of Ellen's purse, the wrapper had slipped off. A very bloody index finger emerged. Several bouts of histrionics followed.

Nurse Mom took one look at the injury and issued orders.

"Here," she said handing Donna the closest clean hand towel. "Wrap your hand with this. Put pressure on the wound with your other hand. Hold it up high."

Dad loaded her into the Aqua Flyer. Doug fired up the new 25, dropped Dad, Donna and Ellen on shore for the 32 km drive south to Kingston General Hospital.

"You'll have to stay out of the water for at least two weeks," ordered the Emergency doctor. Upon her return to the island she begrudgingly announced I could now move ahead one notch in the learn-to-water-ski queue.

Two days later there I was. Knees like jelly, arms stretched almost free of my shoulder sockets, fingers vice-gripped to the bar of the towrope. Magically I had made it to a standing position on top of the water. I skimmed the surface, desperately struggling to keep the water skis parallel, and the pointed in the same direction. Flying.

"You're up." Mom yelled encouragement from the swimming rock. Roger, barked frantically at this new terrifying activity. Donna smiled weakly, secretly glowering, shooting a few daggers.

"Hang on," Doug shouted, from his spotter position in the backseat. Dad was at the wheel. It had taken me two days of practice to get to this point. Of course I was going to hang on. I started to feel comfortable. Time to take a chance. I had seen Doug cross the wake. How hard could it be? I leaned a bit to the left. My short, slender feet strained to maintain grip, swimming inside the floppy, one-size-fits-all white rubber bindings. Too much lean. The clunky five-foot long, half-inch thick Peterborough water skis shot crazily out to the right. I let the tow bar slip out of my fingers. My face slammed into the churning white water of the wave.

For those few brief seconds I had become Esther Williams, waterskiing star of *Easy to Love*, my favourite 1940s movie extravaganza, filmed in Florida's Cypress Gardens. Gone was my dorky white chin-strapped rubber bathing cap and faded hand-me-down crinkle-cotton blue bathing suit. I stood tall and glamorous, resplendent in a coral form-fitting suit. Thanks to my over-active imagination, I also had the figure to fill it out. A sparkling tiara crowned my golden curls. A silk scarf fluttered gracefully behind me as I effortlessly criss-crossed the wake, trailed by a phalanx of Hollywood-handsome, muscular male skiers.

The entire family learned to water ski that summer. Even Jamie and Mom. Dad manned the controls, right hand on the gearshift, a position he would selflessly assume for several hours almost every afternoon for many summers to come. A university star quarterback and summer canoe guide, Dad valued the importance of outdoor athletics. Mom excelled at tennis, swimming, singing and dancing. There was never any question: we would all become skilled at water skiing, as we had become adept at rowing, paddling and swimming.

Dad and Doug learned at the same time. Dad experimented with the technique of driving the boat and Doug with learning to ski. Dad assumed his position at the helm of the Aqua Flyer. Doug bobbed in the water, floating head up with the aid of a bulky orange kapok life jacket we all had to wear, working to keep the skis vertical and parallel in front of him. That first day after first making a smooth pass around Doug with the ski rope, Dad motored slowly ahead stretching out the rope until the handle bobbed up near Doug's hand. Almost simultaneously Doug had to reach for the bar, fight to keep the buoyant wooden skis almost vertical, thread the tow line between the ski tips, wait for tension on the line, then call out over the sound of the idling motor. "Ready."

Donna glumly spotted, keeping her eyes on the skier from the back seat of the boat. Dad made several tries, experimenting to figure out how much forward throttle was needed to get Doug smoothly up out of the water. The first few times Dad blasted Doug forward out over the skis. The next few he used too little thrust. Doug, determined to hang on, submarined until his arms gave out.

"One more try, then that's it for the day," Dad called.

Ready," shouted Doug.

Bingo. The next attempt worked. Doug's slim frame burst onto the surface. He was flying. The crowd on shore cheered. Roger barked. Even Donna cracked a smile.

Second mortgage negotiated, the island officially ours, Dad had celebrated, splurged with Doug's help, on the boat and skis. Water skiing soon became the all-encompassing focus of our lives.

If you had asked me how things were that summer, I would have said, "Perfect."

That was until Dad received a startling letter from the tax department.

CHAPTER 28
FLOATING INTO THE FUTURE

August 2021

*B*arry steps out onto our island dock. I stand up in our double rowing station rowboat. No flat bottom like Grandpa's boat. It's tippy.
"Okay. Give me a hand."

It's my 75th birthday. We are returning from an evening in Kingston. I've enjoyed a glass of wine with dinner and I'm wearing a dress for the first time this summer. Male members of our extended family know I prefer to disembark from boats independently. In this instance I acquiesce. I try to use his hand for a bit of balance only. Stable balance is a crucial asset when you live on an island with uneven ground and gently shifting floating docks.

I'm almost asleep later that night in bed when Barry asks. "How old was your Mom when she first noticed problems with her balance?" I turn toward him. His frown, partially illuminated by moonlight, shows concern.

"Dad said they first noticed it when she was about seventy-five. She started to trip while playing tennis. When it happened too often, she went to the doctor."

A loon calls in the distance. Then silence. No doubt the age coincidence troubles us both. "Now you know why I insist on getting in and out of boats on my own."

When we arrived at the island this year, having missed one

summer season due to Covid-19, I felt oddly tentative getting in and out of boats. After a few days, my sea to land to sea balance returned.

"You know, they didn't tell us about the Parkinson's diagnosis until two or three years later, sometime in 1993, when it became obvious something was wrong. As usual, they didn't want to worry us," I say.

Despite Mom's increasing lack of muscle control and related balance issues my determined parents continued to spend at least four months on the island every summer. In 1998 when Mom needed a wheelchair, Dad bought a used pontoon boat so Mom could enjoy what turned out to be her last summer at the cottage. Except for a few birthday cruises, they used it to ease Mom's movement on and off the island.

Mom and Dad always led by example, never preaching, just gently showing the way. When Mom died in 2000, Dad, well into his eighties, promptly sold the floating necessity.

"What was it Dad said when you met him at the dock on shore that time? You were loading lumber into the aluminum boat. Was he in his new rowboat?" I ask.

I could hear the smile in Barry's voice. "No. He was in that canoe he bought at Frontenac Outfitters, after he sold the pontoon boat. He told me it was a great day for a paddle. I got the hint."

The next summer we bought stand up paddle boards. Race boards. Great for working on balance for winter skiing. Over the years we assembled our own fleet of canoes, kayaks and rowboats.

It may be the aging demographic of Draper Lake cottagers, or might well be the influence of pandemic staycation guidelines. This year five pontoon boats regularly cruise the waters of the lake. Some for early morning fishing expeditions, some to accommodate aging knees and some for happy hour or sunset cruises.

I'm not ready for a pontoon boat yet. Blessed with good genes and a modicum of inherited athletic ability I'm holding out until I need one. At least, that's what I tell myself those mornings when I wake up with stiff muscles. Searching for self-discipline I usually *persevere enough to amble down the path, carry my stand up paddle board to the lake and step off the dock for a morning turtle hunting expedition.*

It's inevitable. Our time will come. Hopefully well into our ninth decade. Until then, I refuse to take a hand getting out of the boat.

CHAPTER 29
CAMPFIRE LEGACY

1956

"The night is cold and wet, but in the tiny parlour of Laburnum Villa on the misty moors of the English countryside the blinds are drawn and the fire burns brightly. Mr. White and his son Herbert are engrossed in a game of chess. Mrs. White knits by the fire."

A spellbinding storyteller, the Reverend Ted Leighfield hesitated, staring over the glowing red embers of the campfire. He leaned forward, hands resting on his knees, then locked eyes, one by one, with each of the children and adults in the circle. Slowly, deliberately, he turned his head, including each person, drawing them into the story. He explained the Whites are expecting a guest but despair of him appearing.

"The pathway's a bog and the road's a torrent in their out-of-the-way location. Finally, the gate bangs loudly and heavy footsteps approach the door."

My fingers ached from gripping the wooden bench Dad had moved from the table indoors. My shoulders hunched against the charcoal-dark night, muscles taut with anticipation from holding my breath. Who would darken the door of their remote cottage?

As Mr. Leighfield continued, he conjured the image of the expected family friend, a tall burly man with beady eyes, Sergeant-Major Morris, who has returned from a twenty-one-year military posting in India. Mr. Leighfield's rasping tones invited us to follow the visitor along a dim hallway into the parlour as the family welcomes him, eager to hear his tales of distant lands and strange people.

Our campfire leader then paused and took a leisurely sip from his glass.

"After the third whiskey the sergeant's eyes grow brighter and he regales them with his exploits and a mysterious monkey's paw he has brought back with him."

Equally eager and terrified to discover what powers lay within the mummified monkey's paw brought from India by the mysterious Sergeant-Major Morris, I clung to the security of the bench.

My love affair with storytelling and fascination with the mysteries of the Orient began that night with Ted Leighfield's campfire version of W.W. Jacob's 1902 story – The Monkey's Paw.

The morning of the campfire Dad sat on the edge of my bed.

"If there's no wind or a light, offshore breeze tonight, we'll invite the Leighfields and cottagers from the mainland for a campfire."

I stepped out of bed. The ochre floorboards felt cold and gritty under my bare feet. The hand-stitched red gingham curtain slid smoothly along its wire as I pulled it aside. The feathery needles of the sentinel Eastern White Pines guarding the middle of our island stood as still as Busby-topped soldiers guarding Buckingham Palace. No wind. The pewter sky promised precipitation. Would it rain, dampen our island to Dad's specifications, then clear in time? I dove back under the covers. The red and black Hudson's Bay blanket weighed heavily against the chill of the late August morning. Eyes tightly scrunched, brow furrowed in concentration, I made a wish tonight would be the night.

Electricity still hadn't reached our island. No TV, no CBC radio. The internet beyond our imagination. The last campfire before school started in September promised to be the social highlight of the season.

We had hoped, for seemingly endless days, for the perfect conditions. Dad said the island had to be drenched by rain. During the day we inspected the cedar needles, maple and oak leaves to check if they were moist enough to withstand errant sparks. We hoped it was safe enough for a campfire. That evening the breeze drifted almost imperceptivity in an offshore direction. Flying embers would almost certainly fly toward the lake, away from the towering brush pile. The results of several weeks of clearing, the pile of dried branches was a skyscraper, well above Dad's head.

All summer we had longed for the appearance of our revered storyteller, Ted Leighfield, a United Church minister whose family owned Turkey Island. About a ten-minute row from us, we could see their island clearly from our swimming rock. By day we shared our front swimming rock with the five Leighfield kids. By night, at our infrequent campfires, they shared their Dad with us. Mr. Leighfield spent most of the summer at Five Oaks, a United Church Camp in Paris, Ontario, where he acted as Associate Director and resident raconteur. This Labour Day weekend he was all ours.

We remembered bits of his story from previous campfires.

Mr. Leighfield informed us of Mr. White's desire to go to India himself, to wander the dusty streets among the old temples, meet the *fakirs* and jugglers and hold in his hand the paw the sergeant had mentioned earlier. Our barrel-chested campfire leader slowly raised his hand in a clenched fist, mimicking the shape of the paw. We could almost feel Mrs. White's body stiffen and see her ashen face. Mr. Leighfield regaled us with the gruesome details of how, when the sergeant-major took the paw out of his pocket to show, Mrs. White drew back with a horrified grimace. Mirroring her horror, we all drew back in delicious fear.

"Mr. White again expresses an interest in going to India,

but the sergeant-major explains he would be better off staying at home," Mr. Leighfield continued. Why, we wondered? We longed for details. What could happen in India?

Campfire preparations started late afternoon. We helped Mom set out the long table, an industrial metal door with four legs attached. Donna and I set out plastic jugs and clear juice glasses with blue flowers. Mom sent Doug into the woods to cut fresh sucker branches from a large basswood tree for marshmallow roasting sticks. "Make sure they're really long. Don't want to have to get too close to the bonfire, Mom said. All I could think about was the story to come. Shivers of anticipation washed over me each time we heard about India and the monkey's paw.

We recalled some sort of magic spell put on the paw by an old fakir, a holy man, who wanted to show that fate ruled people's lives and those who interfered with it did so at their own sorrow. The secret of the paw, Mr. Leighfield had explained, captivating our imagination each time, was that the *fakir* put a spell on it so that three separate men could each have three wishes from it.

Doug sank into a camp chair, strung with sagging green webbing, took out his pen knife and whittled one end of each roasting stick to a clean sharp point. Dad filled three galvanized pails with lake water. He placed them close to the brush pile in case flames flared in the wrong direction. He gathered a few short cedar and birch logs from his woodpile and placed them by the pail, ready to pile on the coals to create a peaceful red glow for the late evening campfire.

At dusk as beavers silently slipped away from their lodges for nighttime forays, rowboats, motorboats and canoes pulled up to our dock. Just before dark Dad removed a box of wooden Eddy matches from his shirt pocket, shook one loose and struck the red tip on the rock. He stooped over slightly and threw the burning match into the soaring, tightly packed pile of interwoven cedar branches.

"Stand back, everybody. It's going to be a hot one."

Dried brush ignites dramatically in the blink of an eye. Whoosh. Sparks shot skyward, mimicking the sound of a jet engine, then flitted like fireflies above the heat of the flames to mingle with the stars. Mom kicked off the evening in her strong contralto.

"Fires burning, fires burning
Draw nearer, draw nearer
In the gloaming, in the gloaming
Come sing and be merry."

She followed immediately, leading a rousing chorus of
Hail, Hail the gang's all here

Everyone joined in, unfolded their chairs and settled in a circle around the fire. The kids got out the sticks and roasted marshmallows, then squished the gooey mesh between graham crackers spread with peanut butter. Chocolate was too expensive.

Sticky from S'mores washed down with lime Freshie, we squatted down on the swimming rock, rinsed our gooey faces and fingers in the lake, then returned to the fire ring.

Mr. Leighfield rose imperiously at the edge of the circle, raised his muscular arms as he called out in a deep baritone, honed by many hours in the pulpit. "Who wants to go on a "Lion Hunt?"

His bulky frame and dark eyes materialized in the glow of the campfire. He seemed like the exotic midnight stranger of his story.

Going on a lion hunt,
Gonna catch a big one

We followed the familiar lackadaisical hand and foot gestures as the hunt progressed. When we crept virtually into the darkness of the cave, we came face to face with the shiny eyes, cold nose and dark teeth of the lion. Suddenly the escape route picked up speed. Standing in place, we swished back through the grass with our palms, flailed our arms to mimic swimming across a pond, stomped our feet as if running around a tree and raced into the house, slammed the door, bounced our knees up and down to simulate running up the stairs and pretended to hide under Mom's bed.

Gasping for breath, lungs on fire after our flight from the lion, we mustered up enough energy to coax Mr. Leighfield to tell the scariest story we knew.

"Let's hear *The Monkey's Paw*. C'mon. You promised".

We huddled under the warm wings of our parents as he pulled his lawn chair forward ready to draw out every terrifying detail of the story of the evil talisman.

My cheek cuddled against the worn fabric of Dad's plaid shirt.

"The Sergeant-Major has considered selling the paw, but he doesn't want it to cause any more trouble than it already has," Mr. Leighfield continued.

He enchanted us with tales of Victorian gingerbread-detailed houseboats on Dal Lake in Srinigar, Kashmir. We visualized the red mud left by monsoon rains, smelled the camphor and dampness of the houseboat interiors. He carried us along the route of the ancient Himalayan Queen express mail train, past fragrant frangipani and giant rhododendron, as it snaked its rickety way upward beside icy foothills to the multi-coloured houses clinging to the mountains above Shimla. We sipped lemon ginger tea on the verandah of the Viceregal Lodge, residence of the British viceroy of India.

We cringed as Mr. Leighfield's hand pulled a small, black box from his jacket. He detailed the spell placed on the hairy, shriveled appendage by the *fakir*. "Whoever owns the paw will be granted three wishes. But it also contains a curse, a malediction to prove people's lives are governed by fate, and it is dangerous to meddle with fate."

We'd heard the story before. I could never remember the exact ending. As a result, it held the power to horrify me again and again. We leaned in, relishing in the security of our inner circle. Entranced by the oldest art in the world, *hakawati*, the ancient Arab art of storytelling, we huddled like tribesmen in an oasis camp. Gathered not amid desert sands, we were isolated by the surrounding dark jade liquid of the lake. A sea of fiery crystals, the brilliant stars mirrored in the lake, enchanted us.

Mr. Leighfield rose and stretched, then casually tossed a piece of kindling on the fire. At the same time he told how the Sergeant-Major threw the paw into the fireplace, then snatched it back. From nowhere he produced the black box again, demonstrating exactly how Mr. White quickly rescued the paw and had asked to be told how to make the wishes. He then explained how White, warned to use common sense, decided to wish for two hundred pounds, the amount of money due on the mortgage of their house.

"As Mr. White utters the wish out loud the paw writhes like a snake in his hand and he sees a vividly realistic monkey face in the flames." Mr. Leighfield then silently opened the box on his knees and produced what looked like a claw shaped, hairy appendage. Some laughed. Not me. Every time he reached this part I shivered and checked the fire for ape-like visages.

We felt Mrs. White's apprehension as she peered out the window at a well-dressed stranger pausing at their gate who finally flings open the gate and walks up the path and knocks on the door. She invites him in.

"At first he is strangely silent," Mr. Leighfield explained. We all wondered who it could be.

"The visitor announces himself as a representative of Maw and Meggins, the factory where their son Herbert works," he contnues. We shuddered at the news of a terrible accident. It seems Herbert was caught in the machinery but felt no pain. Does that mean Herbert's all right, we wondered, afraid to ask. Mr. Leighfield stared into the night past the faces glowing in the firelight.

"He presents the Whites with two hundred pounds as compensation for the death of their son."

Our narrator paused for a drink of water, giving us time to consider the folly of wishing for money. Mosquito-hunting bats swooshed overhead, fireflies danced through the branches behind us. The moon stretched a pale yellow pathway across the lake. Dad added a cedar log to the fire. It crackled, accentuating the stillness of the moment.

The storyteller's somber tone carried us to the graveyard where, exhausted and hopeless, the Whites lower the wooden box carrying their son into the damp ground. We are invited again, one week later, into the cozy parlour. Mrs. White demands they use the monkey's paw to wish Herbert back to life. We witness a heated argument, and cringe. Mr. White tells him how Herbert's body was so badly mangled it could be identified only by the clothes.

"But Mrs. White insists. He makes the wish. As they wait, the candle goes out."

At this point I was no longer able to sit still. The image of Herbert's body caught in the machinery was too much. I winced at the thought of the ruthless blades of the machine. After Donna's leg shaving injury, sharp objects, particularly razor blades, made my stomach queasy. Often, in storytelling less is more, suggestion stronger than blatant description, images conjured in the brain the most powerful creations.

Silence followed. Our host stared past us as if seeing the scene unfold somewhere across the black lake. Moments later, Mr. Leighfield rapped his knuckle on the wooden arm of his Muskoka chair. Then again, more insistent.

We hung on every word, eyes glued to his face, stained orange by the firelight. Afraid to look behind us, our gaze focused on the black pawlike lump now resting in his lap. He closed his eyes, drawing out the suspense, inhaled slowly and continued.

His furrowed brow and frantic eyes helped us imagine Mr. White's desperation as he begs his wife not to open the door. Mr. Leighfield then grasped the paw tightly, raised it dramatically against the ebony starlit sky.

"Just as she pulls back the bolt, he grabs the paw and makes his final wish. The knocking stops."

Silence again.

"He opens the door to an empty doorstep."

"What happened? Was anybody there? Who got the paw next?" we called out. Those were his final words. He left us guessing about the conclusion.

The red coals paled to embers. We settled back as the campfire drew to an end. Weaving a magical tale seemed effortless for Mr. Leighfield. His carefully chosen and artfully delivered words seized my attention. His envious gift of keeping members of our multi-aged gathering transfixed by his words and gestures never left me.

And so the night ended. We watched, transfixed, as the master storyteller ceremoniously placed the paw back in its box. Silently he slipped the box back into his jacket. We were never allowed a closer look.

Evening campfire with niece Sherri McFarlane and her husband Paul Tesssier at the front swimming rock 2021. —Patti Shales Lefkos

CHAPTER 30
ORIGIN OF A
STORYTELLER

November 2011

I *remove my dusty hiking boots and place them beside the rows*
of brown plastic flipflops left by the monks. Steps inside the
monastery in the remote Solo Khumbu province of Nepal I
approach the rustic case with a healthy amount of skepticism. I
lean toward Barry. I try to speak softly enough not to offend the
young novice monk who has unlocked the heavy wooden door to
allow us into the viewing area.

"What do you think? Real?"

The glass case locked with a golden padlock, sits on a waist-high
pedestal. An ancient monk approaches. He dramatically draws
aside a white Buddhist khata scarf to unveil a shriveled mound
that looks like a scalp. Through the dusty glass I can make out the
conical-shaped object. It appears to be a brown hide adorned with
orange-brown hair that could be from an ape, bear or even a yak.

"Apparently it was found by Sir Edmund Hillary and journalist
Edmund Doig in 1960." Barry raises his eyebrows slightly, head
still close to mine.

Out of nowhere a shiver runs up my back. I take a step back,
then gather courage and lean in for a closer look. "Kind of creepy."

The plaque above the cabinet describes how Hillary and Doig
found the scalp in the home of an old village woman. She told
them it was a good luck charm for the village and was anxious
about letting it leave. In order to avoid disaster befalling the

village, Hillary agreed to a deal. He would make a donation to the monastery and a local school and then bring along a guardian for the scalp from the monastery so he could take it away and have it examined by archaeology experts in his native New Zealand.

During our tour of Khumjumg village, one of the stops on the Everest Base Camp trek, we have unexpectedly come across this unusual object, purported to be a 300-year-old Yeti scalp. High in the Himalaya, thousands of kilometres from Draper Lake, all I can think of is Mr. Leighfield and The Monkey's Paw. We've been in Nepal for two months, have completed three major treks and are on our way to Everest Base Camp. That memorable moment from my childhood pops inexplicably into my consciousness more than fifty years later.

As I stand in the glow of flickering butter-lamps I marvel at the power of story to transport right back in time to the campfire circle so far from this exotic distant land. It has stayed with me, how family and friends respected Ted Leighfield's ability to mesmerize us with his carefully chosen words and compelling delivery. Even then, secretly I longed to be just like him, the one to hold the group spellbound, the centre of attention, to bask in the warmth of the family circle.

That summer of 1956 was the last time I heard anyone tell "The Monkey's Paw."

"That was the summer I knew I would be a writer," I explain to Barry.

Later that year Mom handed me a cheque, a $100 inheritance from my maternal grandfather, Reverend James Gordon. "It's up to you how you spend it. Just think about buying something important that will stay with you a long time to remember Grandpa."

I bought an avocado green Remington Rand Letter-Riter manual typewriter. It struggled with me through painful attempts at fledgling stories, the bing and swoosh of the carriage

Patti enroute to Everest Base Camp,
Nepal after discovering the yeti scalp 2011. —Barry Hodgins

punctuating every line. I still have those crudely-typed efforts from my early teens. I wrote tales of a United Church minister, who like my grandpa Gordon, funder of the typewriter, warmly welcomed people of different nationalities and financial status, who at the time he deemed less fortunate, into his congregation.

Now I write in my home office surrounded with mementos of the Himalaya, statues of Buddha and of Ganesh, the elephant god widely revered as the remover of obstacles, prayer wheels and temple bells. The horizons of my stories have broadened along with my travel excursions: hiking to the lonely hills of England's Lake District, followed by treks to the base camps of Annapurna and Everest, morning walks with grinning Tibetans in the mystical Shangri-La called Lhasa and the pilgrimage to sacred Mount Kailash on the western wilds of the Tibetan plateau.

Loon Island is still my safe grounding spot, the centre of my universe. Where I can truly be myself, a place to read and satisfy my curiosity about other cultures, a haven to return to after adventures afar. I love to walk barefoot on the pine needle strewn pathway, feel the prickly softness of the sun warmed grass and roughness of the rocks, and know deep in my heart that I am an integral part of a larger ancestral heritage. The closeness of the extended family campfire circle remains, providing the strength and inspiration to continue to wander the mountains of the world in search of the power of stories like "The Monkey's Paw" to hold my imagination.

CHAPTER 31
INVASION FROM BOTH SIDES OF THE BORDER

July 1956

The age gap of four and five years separating me from my older siblings expanded exponentially the night of our first no-parents-allowed campfire. Our family had hosted many island campfire events. It was time for the mainland cottage renters to take a turn. Sometme after a few rounds of hot dogs and s'mores, I felt a change in the ambiance. It was, in fact, right after eight-year-old Sammy Wilson had astonished the gathered throng of blasé teens with his accomplished and totally unexpected rendition of "Que Será, Será." That little song recently made famous by Doris Day initiated our new era of independent campfires. As Sammy sang the final notes my new friend Jennie and I noticed her sister snuggling closer to my brother, moving in for a kiss.

The glow of the fire faintly illuminated the grassy point at the end of the Cedars beach in competition with the waning August moon. Cedar kindling crackled on the fire, mingling with the wood-on-wood symphony of rowboats dancing at the dock in the late evening breeze. I sat cross-legged on the cool ground beside Jennie Miller. Her family had travelled from Rochester, New York for a two-week vacation at the Coolee cottage, third along the shore from the farmhouse. More rustic than the first two structures, the cottage name was inspired by its location. It rested in a lowland drainage area or coolee, a French-Canadian word meaning ' "to flow" '.

"What's your sister doing?" I said.

"I think she's got a crush on your brother."

When Jennie's older sister, blonde, vivacious Helen got one look at my handsome tanned brother it was summer love at first sight, at least on her part. Doug, at fifteen, unaware of his natural charisma, and shy, instantly leaned away, withdrawing from her advances.

Jennie turned away from the fire and looked right at me, peeling the last sticky bits of marshmallow from her fingers and popping them in her mouth. I looked back at her with raised eyebrows and a knowing smirk. Despite our plump prepubescent double digit age status we both tried to appear as if we had a pretty good idea of what was going on.

Doug, Donna and I found the American kids fascinating. Their New York state accents and Hershey Bars seemed incredibly exotic. They accused us of sounding British and peppered us with questions about living in igloos during the winter.

Closest to the farmhouse, the tall Aerie cottage, originally constructed as a boathouse, clung to a wide, steep expanse of granite, falling into the lake. It was now used as guest accommodation. The Wilsons, suburban kids from Rochester, regularly rented there. They were among the first American kids we met.

"There's kids at the Aerie cottage," Doug said one morning on the way back from fetching a block of ice from the farm.

"Did you speak to them?" Mom said. As a minister's daughter and part of the extended family who considered themselves original custodians of the lake, Mom taught us it was our duty to welcome newcomers. Was she teaching us good manners or just wanting us out of the way for a while?

"Go and invite them for a swim this afternoon. Tell them to bring their own towels." Doing laundry in the lake demanded enough energy. She was not about to lend out extra towels.

The Wilsons, friends of the Millers, had claimed two weeks at the Aerie cottage. Soft spoken Harold Wilson, a short, wiry man with an Export A cigarette perpetually dangling from his lip, sought solace from the family ruckus by fishing all day from the red wooden rowboat supplied with the cottage. Mrs. Wilson, almost a head taller, pounds heavier than her diminutive spouse and far more gregarious, captivated our curiosity. She failed to understand how her constant demands on her children to behave better carried across the lake. Every whining word, in what seemed to us a nasal New York state accent, clearly reached our island half a mile away. "Sammy, get off the dock right now. Sammy, get out of the water. Hang up your swimsuit." Or maybe she did understand. Maybe her frustrations got the best of her from time to time and she just wanted to be heard. Sammy usually carried on whatever he was doing, oblivious to her shouts. When that happened, she started in on her older son Jimmy, a contemporary of Donna.

"Jimmy. Get me a pail of water. Those fish your dad caught are stinking up the place. You better clean them before you go anywhere. Go up to the farm and get me a block of ice. The ice box is dripping again."

On and on it went, until sundown. Marianne, the middle child, roamed around the periphery of the family, protecting Sammy and supporting Jimmy.

"Here, Mom. Have another beer. I'll watch Sammy while he's swimming."

Maybe it was the beer. The idea of drinking alcohol during the day, or drinking alcohol at all, scandalized us. As far as I knew at the time, the entire Shales family comprised of strict tee-totalers. Alcohol was never a part of our childhood. Later, when I reached the legal drinking age, Mom and Dad admitted to the occasional alcoholic beverage imbibed secretly to celebrate their wedding anniversaries. Mary secretly divulged the stash of empties in the Wilson's garbage. We felt sad for

Jimmy, Sammy and Marianne, and embarrassed for Mrs. Wilson. I was a bit afraid of her. I'm not sure why. She was always kind and friendly whenever we walked by the Aerie cottage.

Jimmy stood up and threw another log on the fire. About then I caught sight of Donna through the flames on the opposite side of the circle. She sat wedged between two handsome teenaged Americans. On her left, Warren leaned toward her. Everyone called him Brub, a name given to him when one of his younger siblings was unable to pronounce the word brother. The shoulder rubbing hers on her right, belonged to Brub's best friend, Butch. Brub's family was renting the Honeymoon cottage, farthest away from the farmhouse, accessible only by water.

Escapees from the same Rochester suburb as the Wilsons and Millers, Brub's parents loved the seclusion. Seeking friends and excitement, Brub and Butch rowed over to our island the day they arrived. My flirty blue-eyed sister, enthralled by Brub's dark good looks and kindness to his younger siblings and Butch's blond gregarious charm, fell for both of them. Deciding which one she liked best remained her biggest dilemma that summer. Sammy and Jimmy, Jennie and I leaned in close to the fire, lost in our own thoughts. The boys remained quiet. Jennie and I wondered what was going on with our siblings.

That was the night I revealed my first crush to Jennie. That summer I thought I was in love with Kenny Leighfield, one of the kids from Turkey Island. At fourteen, four years older than I, Kenny seemed way too grown up and impossibly sophisticated. My dreams burgeoned with unrequited love. I longed to gently push back the mop of dark hair he wore flopped over his darkly freckled face. Jennie and I invented excuses to go fishing near Turkey Island. I casually invited his sister, Elaine Leighfield, for a swim, hoping she would bring her older brother. I never mentioned the crush to Elaine, terrified she might divulge my secret to Kenny.

Draper Lake no longer existed solely as our private playground. For my first nine summers at Draper Lake, time had stood still. My world consisted of what Mom and Dad could see from the Front Rock, a swath of shoreline from the Cedars cottage to the point beyond our grandparents' island. The exception being occasional forays to Aunt Jessie or Uncle Walter's Bay or a quick trip behind the island to visit Uncle Jack and Aunt Laura. Aunt Gladys remained in residence with our cousins Kenny and David in their cottage on adjacent Huckleberry Island. Uncle Dave joined the family on weekends.

With increased responsibility and seniority, Dad at Canada Life Assurance Company and Uncle Dave at CIL in Montreal, earned the brothers longer vacations. Leaving Reverend Ted behind to manage Five Oaks United Church Camp, tiny but feisty Norma Leighfield corralled her brood of five children in a miniscule cottage on Turkey Island. Uncle Jack and Aunt Laura's adult children Paula, and John, visited frequently. Cousins Donald and Ian vacationed with their grandparents Walt and Hazel.

We welcomed diversions provided by extended family. The Leighfields and American kids became part of our Draper Lake family. Summer days expanded into a glorious haze. We shared boats. We swam island to island. We shared the locations of secret fishing spots. We swapped comics. And, we took turns hosting campfires.

Most afternoons our motley barefoot gaggle of cousins and friends congregated on our front lawn at Loon Island. Sunburned kids and parents arrived in all manner of boats, competing for space in Dad's ever-expanding harbour. Tattered beach towels scattered the granite rock. Carefree kids in faded bathing suits fought for position in the lineup for the diving board. Too hot to wait, some ran down the toe-stubbing granite for a shallow dive. Roger ran up and down the lawn in a frantic attempt to supervise the mayhem. Mom and Dad surveyed the proceedings.

Patti practicing camera technique with a gang
at the front swimming rock. —Will Shales

Refreshed from afternoon tea, Dad revved up the Evinrude
to a steady rumble, threw the Aqua Flyer in reverse and taxied
to the Front Rock to pick up whatever lucky kid had claimed
the spot as first water skier of the day.

Every two weeks a new family arrived, many of them from
Rochester, New York, to rent one of Elwood and Alice's five
cottages. Several members of each of the Rochester families
worked together at Kodak. I pictured them leaning forward
in dimly lit workspaces, squinting through the red glow of
the film processing. Jeannie told me one of their jobs was to
decide which photos revealed too much nudity or vulgarity
for 50s sensitivity and therefore could not be developed. No
one ever told us what happened to those photos. Two weeks
of light and space at Draper Lake must have been a heavenly
escape from Kodak darkrooms.

We rarely saw cousin Mary on cottage turnover weekends.

We loved and admired her and wished she could spend more time with us. Occasionally we caught a glimpse of her carrying buckets of cleaning supplies down from the farmhouse. She emerged hours later and trudged along the beach to clean the next cottage. Later she hauled buckets of fresh lake water to each cottage. She materialized over and over with armloads of freshly chopped firewood to stock the wood box beside each cast iron stove. Shoulders bent, laden with heavy bags of garbage, she tramped back up the hill to the farmhouse. Later she reappeared several more times lugging huge frozen blocks to refill the metal lined chamber in the top of each icebox. Alice, in her 60s by then, swept and cleaned, but the heavy lifting fell to Mary.

The Cedars was the first-choice rental of our Weston neighbours. The Montgomerys, Gord and Eloise, belonged to the same bridge club as Mom and Dad. Mom and Eloise were best friends. We called them Aunt Eloise and Uncle Gord. The two housewives carpooled to the Weston A and P supermarket for grocery shopping, they belonged to the United Church women's group and they regularly gave each other Toni Home Permanents. On those days we arrived home for lunch to be greeted by the acrid stink of neutralizer solution and two mysteriously transformed housewives, heads covered by tightly wound pink curlers, shoulders protected by shiny plastic capes.

Especially when she was on her own with us, Mom loved when the Monties, as we called them, rented a cottage on shore. One of us was often dispatched to pick up Eloise in the rowboat. The two friends enjoyed gossip sessions in the shade, knitting, hand-sewing curtains for the back bedrooms and sipping tea from blue willow cups. Taciturn and distant, Uncle Gord passed endless solitary hours contentedly fishing, rowing and puffing on his pipe. The three of us hosted their kids, Anne and Bill, close in age to Doug and Donna, and baby Jeannie, several years younger than me. Both Aunt Eloise and Jeannie learned to swim at our island, with Dad's patient coaching.

Eloise tentative and Jeannie gleeful, the pair splashed along, hand over hand in the shallow water of our Front Rock.

Cottage life with three kids and countless hangers-on often sent Mom into a tizzy. She enforced strict rules. Weary of constant sweeping, she placed an enamel pan of water on the small porch outside the cottage door. Flat needle-like cedar leaves adhere stubbornly to wet bare feet and Mom was determined to prevent us from tracking cedar detritus into the cottage several times a day.

"Wash your feet outside," she'd yell from the living room. The prevailing winds must often have carried her commands right to Mrs. Wilson. "And, don't leave wet suits and towels on the floor. No comic books until I see your suits on the back line," Mom said.

The resident crew of aunts, uncles, cousins and friends happily swelled to include the Americans. Cottage turnover weekend meant extra chores for Mary. For us, it offered opportunity to meet new friends. For Mom, it signaled the joys and self-imposed challenges of hosting. Whether self-appointed or by default, Dad served as the athletic director. With casual efficiency he programmed croquet, badminton, table tennis and volleyball amid the afternoon roster of swimming, diving and waterskiing. The warmth of our parents and the granite of the swimming rock strengthened Loon Island's reputation as the place to be on a sunny afternoon at Draper Lake.

CHAPTER 32
A VOICE FROM THE PAST

September 2021

"*Hello. Are you Don?" I call from my rowboat.*
The man at the end of the dock turns to face me with a warm smile. I like him already.
"Yes, I am. And you must be Patti."

I row Grandpa's red rowboat closer to the dock. Don walks toward me and sits on one of four Muskoka chairs near the end of the dock. I don't bother to tie up. I figure I won't be there long. I just swing my feet over the edge of the boat so my heels rest on the dock, enough to prevent the boat from wandering.

Doug had told me there were people renting a cottage owned by his daughter Kerry and her husband Barry, who came to the lake when they were kids. "I heard your family used to rent the Aerie Cottage back in the 60s."

He looks familiar. Attired for a cottage afternoon in shorts and a T-shirt topped by a ball cap, he exudes a certain warmth. Still no significant memories jump out at me. Maybe that's because he turned 65 a few days ago. An age span of ten years is huge for the under-twenty crowd. The names of his parents, George and Mary Martin, ring a bell. At one time they were friends of Mom and Dad. Together we figure out his family vacationed at the lake the years I spent summers working as a basket girl and cashier at Weston Area Swimming Pool.

"I remember water skiing and being pulled on a red disk behind Doug Shales' speedboat." A gentle grin accompanies the far-off look in his eyes.

"That would be my dad. The Peterborough Aqua Flyer is still in use. My brother Doug maintains it. It's mostly used for evening cruises now. And that red disk is now the top of a coffee table at the old cottage."

A second man strolls down the dock to join us. "This is my brother Paul." Paul nods and smiles. Hands Don a can beer, damp with condensation.

"Patti tells me this boat is seventy-five years old. It belonged to her grandfather, Will Shales."

The light of a faraway memory shines in Paul's eyes.

"Did it used to be gray, with maroon trim? I think I learned to row in that boat," Paul says. We exchange reminiscences of the Aerie cottage, Elwood, Alice and Mary, the icehouse and campfires. Their wives wander down with fresh drinks.

"How did you guys end up coming to this lake?"

Don, a respected Parliament Hill journalist and former host of CTV news Power Play, and Paul, a lawyer, call Toronto and Ottawa home. But, it turns out both were born in Rochester. "Maybe Mom will remember," Paul says. "She's 93 but still really sharp."

Moments later we hear the voice of their mother, Mary Martin, on speakerphone. "A nursing colleague in Rochester told me about Draper Lake."

Mystery solved we lean into the phone as she regales us with tales of times with my Mom and Dad and grandparents. Years melt away. Right on cue a loon calls to greet her before we say good-bye.

I begin to push my rowboat from the dock and say goodbye when Paul asks, "Would it be okay to have a row in your boat?"

"Sure," I say, and mention a few tips about the fragility of the ancient oarlocks.

I step out of the boat and Paul steps in. We push him away from the dock. The grin of a nine-year-old spreads across his face as he rows in a wide circle. He still knows how. His wife raises her phone to video the occasion. Slowly he edges Grandpa's rowboat back along the dock, one of many past visitors reluctant to let go of a part of their childhood in this magical place.

CHAPTER 33
THE SWEET BREEZE OF CHANGE

1958

The summer of 1958 Doug turned 17. His muscles still held memories of previous springs and summers of hauling heavy bags around the well-manicured fairways and greens of the Weston Gold Club. He longed for some other form of part-time employment. He knew Mom and Dad expected him to get a summer job.

"I really wish I could spend the summer at the lake."

Dad didn't miss a beat. "Why not ask Elwood if he needs a hand at the farm. He might pay you a bit."

Doug didn't waste any time. He went right to the kitchen and dialed the operator and asked to be connected to the farm. "Inverary, two-five, ring-five, please," he said. Elwood picked up the receiver hanging from the wall of the farmhouse kitchen. "Sure. I could do with two extra hands. Do you have a friend you can bring? Two dollars a week plus room and board. That's my final offer."

"I'll take it," Doug said.

In early July, Doug settled into the childhood single bed of our Grandpa Shales. Doug's high school buddy, Rick Gogo, sank into the adjacent soft mattress. The boys slouched along the slats of the steel bed frames belonging to the identical twins,

Elwood's barn built in 1881. —Barry Hodgins

our Grandpa Will and his brother Walter, and dreamt about the summer to come. Dawn came early that first day, especially for two teenaged boys just finished a year of high school. Soon after the crow of the first rooster, Aunt Alice dished up a hearty breakfast. To prepare workers for the day Alice served farm fresh eggs with home-cured ham followed by homemade bread toasted and slathered with generous dollops of her own raspberry jam. In the early light of dawn Doug and Rick trailed wearily after Elwood, Mary and Alice along the dirt road to the barn.

Elwood looked back over his shoulder. "Whenever you find a farm gate closed, close it again behind you."

Lesson number one.

Elwood milked thirteen cows by hand. Mary opened the barn door and called out ' "So Bossie" ', the customary manner of addressing diary cows at the time. Three velvety brown jersey cows, who seemed to sense their superiority based on the richness of their milk, led the parade, regal heads held high.

Ten scruffy black and white Holstein sisters fell in behind in an orderly fashion. Full udders swaying, the docile beasts swished the frayed ends of their ropey tails, aimed at the crowds of black flies gathered on their hindquarters. Hooves straining for purchase and stability on the slippery cement floor, they trod gingerly over the trough to their individually assigned stanchions. Mary's tall rubber boots protected her from the sprays of bovine urine and scattered cow patties. She squeezed between their heads, hand over hand, stopping at each face to close the iron bars that held them in place.

Elwood and Mary positioned themselves on battered three legged stools. Each leaned a left cheek forward against the cow's flank, grabbed the teats and got down to business. The cows recognized a familiar touch, stayed calm. The ping of milk on the bottom of the metal pails rang at first, followed by a rhythmic sloshing as the pail filled. Elwood and Mary milked three cows in the time it took Doug to persuade one of them to part with half a pail full. Rick, who had never visited a farm before, looked on in awe. It would be a few days before Rick gathered enough nerve to lend a hand.

Humming absentmindedly, Aunt Alice hovered over the meticulously sterilized separator. When not in use, she kept it covered with cheesecloth secured with wooden clothes pegs. Despite her thin cotton sleeveless housedress, the morning humidity took its toll. Beads of perspiration dribbled past wisps of greying hair barely contained by her cotton kerchief. Decades of daily dawn-to-dusk labour had bent her back, bowed her legs slightly and calloused her hard-working hands. Mary raised the heavy pails of milk with arms muscled from eighteen relentless years of farm chores. In a smooth measured motion she poured the milk through the cheesecloth. Rick and Doug took turns rotating the crank by hand and steadying glass milk and cream bottles as they filled from the spout above. Under Alice's watchful eye not one drop of milk was wasted.

During the summer Elwood could occasionally afford to hire

extra help. The remainder of the year the family of three tackled the endless chores required to eke a living out of a farm located within the challenging and often unforgiving conditions, long winters and scant soil, of the Canadian Shield. Mom explained how our cousin Mary came to be an only child. "Aunt Alice apparently lost twins at birth. Stillborn, I think. Identical twin boys, just like your Grandpa and Uncle Walt."

I felt sad for Mary, often left on her own. She worked so hard every day, She often had to leave early from afternoon swim time with us on the island, if she got there at all, to go and get the cows for evening milking.

So without siblings for help and company Mary learned to perfect every manner of farm chore. Despite a petite frame she developed into a slim, well-muscled, extremely reliable woman who could do the work of several men. Her strength and skill, along with the expectations of her parents and the myriad responsibilities of farm life, astonished me. Our winters in the suburbs and summers on the island seemed so uncomplicated and ideal by comparison.

In July Uncle Elwood concentrated on getting the hay inside the barn. The five or six fields of hay close to the barn ripened before the other crops. "Gotta get it in at the right time. Want it to taste good for the animals next winter. So far we've been lucky with the weather."

There was always the chance rain could ruin it. "Wet hay makes hot hay. Can't afford a barn fire."

By the time Doug and Rick arrived to start their summer sojourn Uncle Elwood had already led his handsome Clydesdale pair, Ted and Daisy, up and down the hayfields many times, hitched up first to the mower, then the hay rake. The boys arrived in time for the next step in the process.

"I drive the horses. You walk along beside the wagon, pitch the hay up to me. I'll pile it up here on the wagon. Pitch it clean. Get it all. Don't waste any."

Two city boys with soft hands unaccustomed to labouring

long hours in the sun got a rude awakening. Each time they raised the pitchfork overhead, itchy bits slipped inside their sweaty shirts. They soon removed their sticky shirts, now more an irritant than a comfort. Every few rows Elwood tightened the reins to bring Ted and Daisy to a halt. After taking a swig Elwood passed a milk bottle full of water down to the boys. Already shirtless in dusty overalls he gazed at the completed section. He noticed the leaves of the maples lining the field shudder gently, "What a sweet breeze."

Once the level of hay topped the height of the wagon ladder Ted and Daisy hauled the load to the barn. The boys walked behind. Elwood steered the horses around to the back of the barn where he guided the full load inside. Next, he unhitched them and led them back outside to be hooked up to the hay fork ropes.

" Okay. Now push the hay fork down into the load," Elwood instructed the boys. "Pull the claws closed to grab the hay." Elwood's weathered hands skillfully directed Ted and Daisy. The hay fork travelled up toward the ceiling of the barn, across the open haymow to the correct spot. "Now, pull the tripline."

Once executed, the hay fell magically into the storage space in the barn. "That's way easier than pitching it all by hand. Five more forkfuls until the wagon's empty." After the first round let go, Rick scratched his itchy, sunburned back. "Then we're out in the sun again."

Mealtime routines established the first day rarely varied all summer. At the farm table the noon meal mirrored our family's idea of evening dinner. Aunt Alice weighed down the kitchen table with a hearty array of meat and vegetables accompanied by warm bread or rolls fresh out of the woodstove. A large jug of fresh well water stood next to a smaller metal vessel of maple syrup, both permanent fixtures on the kitchen table. Twirling strips of sticky flypaper stretched down from the ceiling, weighted with insect carcasses, sometimes still wiggling.

After noon dinner it was back to the hayfields for more hours in the punishing sun until time for evening milking. Mary knew the farm, every sumac, maple and oak grove, each hill and hummock and every hidden pasture the cows preferred. Doug and Rick wandered behind, sometimes for hours, often stopping on a rise called the Listening Hill. Enjoying the surrounding vista, they waited for the distant tinkle of the cowbell that would lead them to the entire herd. Once found, udders bursting, the cows contentedly swayed their way back to the barn under Mary's direction.

At the evening meal the boys enthusiastically inhaled a second substantial dinner and savoured the addition of fresh-out-of-the-woodstove-oven raspberry or blueberry pie. Conversation was sparse, often punctuated by Uncle Elwood's low rumble, "Pass the syrup."

It was his habit to smother both main course items and dessert with his own syrup. He earned it by spending chilly spring mornings driving Ted and Daisy as they pulled the sled through snowy sugar-bush woods to the sugar shack. There he tended a constant fire under the pan of sap to reduce the sap to a tasty, sweet syrup. Any discussion of chores halted at precisely 6 p.m. when the farm report came on the radio, giving the price for livestock, cattle, pigs and horses. Ten minutes later the scrape of wooden chairs sounded as they were pushed away from the table. Mary poured hot water into a galvanized pail from the huge black kettle perpetually on the boil on the woodstove and led off to the barn for evening milking.

The farm epitomized self-sufficiency. Some evenings Elwood shod the horses, different shoes for summer and winter, in the blacksmith shop beside the house. Elwood, back already bent at the end of a long day in the fields, leaned over to lift Daisy's leg across his leather-aproned thighs to fit the shoes. Each nail hammered in then twisted off as it protruded on the top of the hoof.

After sunset, chickens secure in the hen house, gates closed so the cows stayed close for milking the next morning, Uncle Elwood slumped back to the house. With a loud sigh he retired to the short, lumpy couch in the kitchen for a well-deserved pre-bedtime snooze.

The summer unfolded in a plethora of newly acquired skills, increasingly challenging assignments and wonder at simple yet ingenious methods of simplifying farm chores. The machine house, a framed building behind the barn, housed several simple yet effective farm machines. Doug marvelled at the extended top rail of the gate to the machine house. Elwood had hung a pot of rocks from the end of the extension as a counterweight. The substantial log rail gate always opened and closed with ease.

August days were filled with harvesting grain, oats and wheat. While most of the hayfields ran up to the house, allowing for comfortable lunch breaks in the farmhouse kitchen, the oats flourished in fields a couple of kilometres past the distant back barn. Aunt Alice handed Elwood, Doug and Rick old honey pails full of bread, cheese and apples for the long ride in the empty wagon. Elwood thought it great fun to encourage the horses to speed up over the old bumpy road. Doug and Rick clutched the wagon boards in fear for their lives. Near the back barn Elwood reigned in the horses to a halt beside a wooden trough filled by a spring that ran out of the hillside. The boys ducked their heads in the trough beside the horses sucking up the cool water.

Close by, in a grove of maples, in a six-foot circle fenced off from the cows and horses, a spring supplied fresh drinking water for the farm crew. "You would lie on your stomach and drink the beautiful, cool water, sometimes poking a frog out of the way," Doug said.

At the bottom of a steep hill, just before reaching the back oat fields, Elwood yanked on the reins, stopping Ted and Daisy for a moment. "Time to hitch up the drag sled contraption. We'll haul it to the top of the hill."

Once at the top Elwood instructed the boys to unhitch the device on the roadside. On the return trip they attached it to the back wheels of the wagon. It prevented the horses from being pushed down the steep hill by the heavy load of grain.

"Simple, but ingenious." Elwoood grinned as he drove the horses slowly downhill.

The ever-present threat of rain challenged the grain harvest. The multi-step process began as the grain was cut then pulled across a canvas table. The stalks were then fed into the binding machine that wrapped, tied and bundled the sheaves and spit them out on the other side. "You boys walk behind, pick up each sheaf, then lean them against each other into stooks. Tomorrow we'll fork the sheaves onto the wagon."

The penultimate process was delivering the heavy wagon load along the potholed road to the main barn to await the arrival of the threshing machine in the fall. "Early day tomorrow. Let's get these stooks loaded before the rain or we'll have to open them up and wait another day or two."

On the rare occasion rain prevented farm chores Doug and Rick had the day off and were allowed to go fishing. "Bring me back a catfish," Alice would say. "You know it's my favourite."

Once a week Elwood piled the boys into the old sedan. It remained in the drive shed most of the time, reserved for picking up general farm supplies like bags of pig feed or more formal Sunday excursions to Perth Road United Church. Dust clouds exploded from the seats at each bump along the road to The Corners in Perth Road Village. The boys sidled up to Charlie Hughson's long wooden counter to splurge part of their $2 weekly wage on comic books, gum, pop and ice cream cones.

For Doug and Rick summer ended all too soon. The day before the boys returned to the suburbs for their Grade13 year at Weston Collegiate and Vocational School Elwood slipped them each a bonus ten dollar bill. He shook their hands with gratitude and tears in his eyes.

"I'll never forget that moment," Doug says now. "I look back and realize that was the last summer Elwood used horses to pull the machines and do the heavy work. The tractor took over the next year. I was fortunate to experience some farm history firsthand. I wish I could do it all over again."

That summer cemented in Doug's bones and muscle the Shales fierce attachment to the land, a sense of belonging and loyalty passed down from Elwood's great grandfather John Harbor Shales Senior. Elwood's insistence on holding on to the family farm when Frontenac Provincial Park was proposed and developed, ensured the legacy and commitment to the land that continues to this day. Grandpa never mentioned whether Elwood was offered money from the government. It wouldn't have made any difference. He would never have parted with the land. Recently, Cousin Mary overheard her daughter, Wendy Newport, in conversation with her sons during a visit to the farm. "When I'm gone you'll inherit the farm. You have to promise me, you must promise me, you will never sell."

Every summer on the island was different. When we were tenting time seemed to stand still. Nothing changed. Then Dad built the cottage. Summers got longer. Eventually the four- and five-year span separating me from my siblings that had earlier seemed irrelevant, expanded in significance. The summer of 1958 when Doug worked on the farm we hardly saw him except for the occasional late afternoon swim and water ski. These interludes were often interrupted by the clang of a cowbell from the distant shore when Doug, Mary and Rick would take off to fetch the cows. When Donna's friend Ellen visited, the two of them dove headfirst into magazines, consuming endless hours with hushed discussions of boys, lipstick, Clearasil, poodle skirts and saddle shoes.

Left alone to hang around home base, I caught snippets of Mom and Dad's conversations about cottage taxes. Never one to part with his hard-earned cash easily, Dad had started another correspondence, this time with Canada Revenue. "I wrote them a letter," he said, more than once. "I told them we shouldn't have to pay so much. The cottage isn't complete. I've only built a screened-in porch, so far. That last letter should hold them for a while."

Mom would roll her eyes, mentally calculating how the tax bill might affect her weekly allotment of grocery money from Dad. She suspected they'd have to pay what was originally asked every year from then on.

CHAPTER 34
LONG DISTANCE CALLING

April 2021

SilverStar Mountain Resort

*I*t's 7:30 a.m. I've finished my morning latte and toast in front of the fireplace. I'm slouched in the swivel chair in my office off the kitchen. It's time to get down to work. First call of the day is to Doug.

"Hi. Are you on a break?" I know he's probably busy carving cherry wood paddles for his grandchildren. It's 10:30 a.m. in Oakville, Ontario. Once a teacher, always a teacher. Recess breaks are a daily ritual for both of us.

"You up already?" he says.

Doug still loves to tease me. My heart warms at the sound of his voice. We're the only ones left of our nuclear family. The unknowns of Covid-19 prevented our annual summer at Loon Island so it's especially good to connect. Afraid to step into an airplane, Barry and I remained stuck at SilverStar. I know, it's not a bad place to be stuck but in my mind it's a winter place. Summers are for Loon Island; rowing, swimming, paddling followed by tea and happy hour with family.

We enjoyed rambling among the alpine flowers. Barry did some mountain biking and caught up on house maintenance. We tried stand up paddle boarding on Vernon's Kalamalka Lake. But, the constant swarm of powerboats and Ski-doos buzzed way too crazily for my liking. Admittedly, I am spoiled. I love that I am able to walk down the few steps to our dock, unrack my board and launch for a serene turtle-hunting excursion.

"Of course. I was up at 6 a.m. as usual. Already had coffee and breakfast. Just called to thank you for the email. Great details about the summer you worked at the farm." Talking and writing back and forth about long-ago summers somehow helped to ease the pain of missing a summer at the lake.

'Yeah, I've been thinking about it a lot lately. You know, the work never stopped. But, the satisfaction must have been great for Elwood and Alice; your own farm and land, your family pitching in doing various chores. A true team effort," Doug says.

A slightly romanticized memory of a teenager who experienced farm work for only two months more than six decades earlier, I think, but I don't interrupt his reverie. I just listen, looking out at the Steller's jays frolicking, vying for pecking position at the snow-topped bird feeder outside my window.

When he finishes I cut in. "There was one story you left out of your email. Didn't Elwood get you to shoot something? A beaver?" I ask.

"No, it was a porcupine." I can hear the sadness in Doug's voice. "One evening Mary, Rick and I were sitting with Alice and Elwood in the back porch. It was the coolest place at that time of day. Elwood mentioned he had seen a porcupine in the tree behind the drive shed.

"Elwood told me once that porcupines eat the bark in a ring around the trunk. It kills the tree," I say.

Doug continues, "The screen door slammed as Elwood went into the house to get his shotgun."

"He looked back at me through the dark screen and told me to follow him," Doug says. Behind the shed Elwood pointed out a porcupine about seven metres up a tree. "He showed me how to hold the gun, aim and shoot."

His voice almost inaudible Doug says, "So I did. The porcupine fell out of the tree and landed at my feet. It was still alive, but terribly wounded." I wait for Doug to gain composure.

"Elwood picked up a large log and hit it over the head to end the suffering. I have never forgotten that experience. I would never think of doing a similar act again." I don't comment. Just enjoy frolicking Steller's Jays. "But, I know, I was just a city boy not raised to the necessity of killing some animals."

After a pause Doug tells me another story. One about happier times with Elwood. "One time Elwood bought Rick and me chocolate milk at the Perth Road store. He perfectly timed a joke as I drank a big mouthful. I couldn't help myself. When I laughed, the milk squirted out my nose. Elwood grinned back at me. What a mess all over Charlie Hughson's front steps." Doug's tone had changed. The softness of fond memories crept back into his voice.

"You know, we worked dawn to dusk, and fell asleep immediately. I remember thinking each night what a wonderful day it had been, how Uncle Elwood had tried to be humorous and make the work day as much fun as possible."

As Doug talks, I take notes. It's easy to picture Elwood, a faded but clean shirt under his overalls for the trip to Perth Road village.

"Do you think you'll make it to the lake this summer? Doug says.

"I have to. Even if it means walking all the way from BC." I pause in thought. "Maybe we'll drive this year." I wouldn't trade winters at SilverStar for life in Oakville, but I do sometimes envy Doug living so close to the lake.

"I called Mary a few weeks ago. She said the ice was out of the lake. I went down last week, just for the day. Went over to the island and walked by your cottage. "Do you want the good news first, or the bad news?

"I'll take the good first, please," I say.

The trilliums are in bloom beside the path up to your cottage."

"And the bad news?"

"There's a huge pine tree right in front of your cottage, totally dead. If it fell it would smash your roof."

A light dawns. The Ontario border is closed to cottagers, due to Covid travel restrictions, except if they need to access their property for emergency maintenance.

"Send me an email with the info about the tree. Could be our ticket at the border. Listen. I can't miss another year. I'm going to start booking hotels tomorrow. I'll be seventy-five and you'll be eighty this summer. Let's start planning a party at the Front Rock. We'll be there."

CHAPTER 35
LAST SUMMER OF FREEDOM

1959

The knuckles of my left hand whitened as my fingers gripped the steering wheel. My right hand rested gently on the vertical red and white throttle, poised for action. The engine of the 35 hp Evinrude emitted a throaty rumble. Gasoline fumes wafted past my face, stinging my eyes. Aided by a relatively comfortable lifejacket, Dad floated behind the boat at the end of the towrope, ready for takeoff. My friend Jennie, acting as spotter, sat in the seat behind me. She swirled her head from me to Dad and back again. "He looks ready. He's got the bar in his hand. He's waving."

My fingers tightened on the gearshift. Skis parallel, tips breaking the surface, Dad shouted the command. "Gun it."

I gripped the shift and rammed it all the way forward, the way I'd seen Dad do it. "He's up."

I could barely hear Jennie over the roar of the engine. Too scared to do anything else, I kept both hands on the wheel, eyes straight ahead, and concentrated on heading for open water.

For the first time, at age thirteen, I was driving the boat to tow a skier. The challenge filled me with a newfound power and confidence. It made me realize how much Dad believed in me. Or maybe, I thought later, it was because he wanted to be able to ski when Doug wasn't there to drive. In any case, there I was, frantically planning a route to avoid shoreline shallows, sand bars and islands and a course expansive enough to allow for wide gradual turns.

A sudden lurch jolted me back to the present. I dared a quick glance over my shoulder. Dad had crossed the boat wake. He was leaning way out to one side. He headed back across the wake, hesitated in the smooth water behind the boat for a moment. I relaxed. Then, as he leaned out and crossed the wake on the other side, the rope pulled taught. The boat jerked again. Swinging back and forth, he continued transitioning all of his 200 pounds, weight recently gained by hours of desk work imposed by his executive status. The transom, across the stern of the boat, shuddered. Panicked, I wondered if that was supposed to happen. It felt like he was about to yank the transom, along with the lovely new shiny black Evinrude, right off the back of the boat.

I completed a safe wide turn in the open areas near the far shore. Cheers erupted from onlookers as I hauled him past the Front Rock. Then I steered toward the farmhouse shore, frantically hoping to avoid the large sandbar off Grandpa's island and also turn before the long shallow peninsula jutting out from the Cedars cottage beach. Teeth clenched, fingers forcefully curled around the steering wheel, I held my breath and hoped. Tow rope as taut as my biceps, Dad swung smoothly outside the circle then returned to centre as I steered back toward our island. I turned the wheel to direct our path as close to the Front Rock as I dared and cut the motor. Dad let go. He sunk gracefully into the water.

Still trembling, I returned to the dock, happy to let someone else take over. I threw the bowline to Doug waiting on the dock.

"Not bad for a first try, Pretzl," he said.

I hated Doug's nickname for me, but his sly grin erased any momentary irritation. I could tell he was secretly proud of his little sister. Dad handed the dripping PFD to Doug, toweled off of the dock, then stepped back into the boat to reclaim his usual spot at the controls.

"Let's go double. You can have the dry PFD. But I get the long rope," Doug said. He handed me the second lifejacket. "There's another pair of skis on the Front Rock. Kenny and David brought theirs."

These days regulations for skiing with two ropes indicate the rope should be between fifty and sixty-five feet long. We had no idea if there were any rules or special techniques. We experimented to see what worked for us. Dad bought a standard waterski rope in Kingston. We borrowed a second rope from Uncle Dave. Dad tied it off so it was short enough for the short rope skier to pass under the long rope held high by the other skier. The skier on the long rope swung in a larger arc. That person had the responsibility of raising the rope above the head of the short rope skier. Inspired by water ski shows we'd seen at the Canadian National Exhibition we spent endless hours inventing increasingly crazy and, we thought, entertaining doubles routines limited only by the budget for gasoline and Dad's tolerance for time at the wheel.

When shouting over engine noise proved futile, we developed a complicated roster of hand signals. We exhausted all variations of crossing back and forth under the rope, introduced costumes and planned routines with various partners.

It was the summer of 1959. At the lake we remained blessedly oblivious to the world at large. Our crowd wore modest one-piece bathing suits. We gaped at movie magazine photos, awed and somewhat scandalized by provocative images of bikini-clad international sex symbol Brigitte Bardot. Unknown to us, singer Johnny Horton ruled the radio airwaves with "The Battle of New Orleans". Only 90 minutes away in Ottawa Prime minster Diefenbaker shocked Canadians by cancelling the promising jet-fighter interceptor Canada Avro Arrow project due to mounting costs and government restrictions.

It seemed everyone wanted to stay at the lake that summer. American families escaping the bright heat of suburban Rochester and the dark gloom of the Kodak plant settled into the farm rental cottages alongside our Weston neighbours, the Montgomerys. Norma Leighfield and her five kids squeezed into their tiny cottage on Turkey Island. Ted came on weekends when he could get away from camp. Aunt Gladys held the fort with our cousins Kenny and David. Uncle Walter's grandsons, Donald and Ian, secured the guest bedroom with their grandparents. Mary rowed over from the farm when she could be spared. Dad made sure she got an early spot on the water ski roster before she had to go for the cows.

The rest of us blissfully lolled away endless afternoons with badminton, volleyball and croquet competitions interrupted only for afternoon teatime or a chance to wow the crowd with our painstakingly choreographed waterski antics. We started by crossing under the rope back and forth. We upped the ante by pulling off the same maneuver on slalom skis. Next, we added themed costumes. Red plaid shirts and my red straw cowboy hat became sought after accessories. Stunts grew increasingly risky. First we tried two skis, no hands, tow bar tucked behind our knees. Too easy. Next, skiing slalom, we put the free foot behind the bar to the main line, slid the bar up behind one bent knee, raised both hands to wave for the Front Rock sail past. That was when Dad and Mom finally drew the line. Long discussions ensued. Even with Dad driving the boat the adults thought we might slip and be dragged by the boat if we fell. We assured them we'd be fine. From then on we were allowed only to place the bar behind our heel.

Creativity for doubles routines exhausted by the limitations of available equipment and parental restrictions, we coaxed Dad into creating a circular disk a little more than a metre in diameter. We'd seen professional skiers rotating on similar disks. We wanted to give it a try. We found an unused sheet of three-quarter inch plywood under the cottage. Dad hammered a nail in the centre, attached a string and pencil and drew a circle. Doug got out the saw. Sanded and painted white, the disk made the perfect vehicle for learning how to perform 360-degree turns while being towed behind the boat. Dad experimented with speeds for optimum efficiency. Barefoot, no footholds on the slippery surface, we investigated methods to turn the disk and pass the towrope hand over hand behind our back, while balancing to remain upright. The trick, learned after countless tumbles, was to keep the leading edge tilted up in the direction of travel. When that got too easy we put a wooden stool on the disk, not nailed down, so it was possible to sit or stand while turning. The next challenge was to pair one skier with one person on the disk. It took Dad a few tries to ascertain the best speed to keep a skier on the long rope skimming the surface without the short-rope person on the disk becoming airborne in concentric circles.

Big finishes brought bigger cheers. My favourite combination was when two slalom skiers approached the rock, each with a tow bar behind one foot. Next, each removed the rope from behind their heel, stood up straight and executed a graceful arabesque, one leg raised behind, just before letting go of the tow bar. Eat your heart out Esther Williams, I thought. We were certain the Cypress Gardens Waterski extravaganza recruiters would arrive any minute to sign us up.

Having reached what we thought was our limit, we whined for a floating jump ramp. Dad always had some excuse. "Too costly." Dad either couldn't or didn't want to figure out how to build it. "What would we do with it in the winter?"

And, underneath it all, way too dangerous. With no formal lessons, we'd figured out techniques and tricks together. Luckily, we remained unscathed. Mom and Dad wanted to keep it that way. Especially, after Mom and Jamie's experiences.

Tired of missing out on the fun, both Mom and Jamie decided to give waterskiing a try one day. Mom went first. The afternoon started out well enough. Not too much wind, sunny skies. A small crowd of family, friends and Jamie, had gathered on the front lawn. Dad sat at the Aqua Flyer controls; Donna, behind him as spotter. Doug dove in and treaded water beside Mom, offering advice. Jamie and I watched from the Front Rock. Dad steered the boat past Mom, Donna tossed the towrope. Doug grabbed it, let it slip through his hands to nearly the end and handed Mom the bar. With Doug's assistance she brought her feet parallel, ski tips showing above the surface.

"Okay?" Doug said.

Mom nodded.

"Hit it."

Dad gunned the motor. The Aqua Flyer surged forward. Mom, resplendent in her shiny royal blue bathing suit, rose out of the lake.

"She's almost up!" Jamie clapped her hands and wiggled a little dance. Mom leaned left. Then right. Then toppled sideways.

Doug swam out to where she fell. A second round of ski and rope adjustments complete, Dad gunned the motor. She got up farther, wobbled, then fell again.

"Maybe a little faster," Doug advised Dad as he passed by with the rope.

Mom tried again. Same result.

"Not that fast," Doug said on the next pass by.

Not wanting to be outdone by her husband and kids, Mom kept trying. Each time Doug swam after her, farther and farther out into the middle of the lake toward Turkey Island. Mom wore a lifejacket. Not Doug. Close to exhaustion, Doug stayed by her side, treading water, providing encouragement, then swimming after Mom time and time again.

After several more aborted attempts, the giggles consumed them.

"One more go?" Doug burbled, mouth barely above the surface.

Mom nodded, eyes fixed on the horizon.

That's when it happened. Determined to be successful, Mom held on to the rope far too long, and finally fell face forward over the tips of the clunky wooden skis.

Dad reached down and hauled her into the boat. Doug declined to get in.

"I'll swim," Doug said. Then turned, arms bravely stroking

him forward toward the Front Rock in a fast crawl.

They both laughed about it. But, not for long. Whatever the reason, now in her early forties, Mom tended to bruise easily. By evening a rapidly darkening purple oval medal of honour spread across her thigh, from the hem of her bathing suit down to her knee. She wore it proudly. The next evening Jamie sported a matching contusion. After a couple of days of showing off their war wounds and regaling others with stories more hilarious when told than what really happened, Dad discovered the precise lift-off velocity required. They both learned to ski with style and grace. Singles only.

As I think back to that summer a vivid scene forms in my mind. I see a lively montage of family and friends, probably too tanned but healthy, some fully engaged in a ruthless croquet competition, others soaking in the granite warmth of the swimming rock, all unaware of their destinies. They're as yet oblivious to approaching changes in their lives, some sooner than expected.

Jamie didn't come to visit much anymore. She married her farmer fiancée, Ken Tiffen, They operated a trout hatchery north of Toronto and adopted two children. We missed her. Mary wed local boy Wayne Newport and had two daughters. My siblings, early bloomers, rushed ahead, impatient to find mates and start families. None of us could have imagined that only a few years later Donna would marry, deliver her first of four daughters and be working full time in a Weston jewelry store to support Bruce McFarlane, her student husband. Or that Doug would have found the love of his life, Margo Watson, dropped out of an unfulfilling university course, be working for Canada Post and contemplating marriage. A late bloomer, I felt left behind again. By the next summer, when I was fourteen, I would have my first job. Slinging baskets of towels, shoes and clothes into open lockers at the Weston Area Swimming Pool where Doug reigned as head lifeguard was hard work. I longed for time at the lake.

We continued to gather on the front lawn for years to come, but relationships and interests had temporarily shifted. Instead of a gap of four and five years between me and my siblings, for several decades it seemed more like a generation. Our summer world was never to be the same.

They got married, started families and bought homes in Ontario. I attended classes at the University of Toronto, taught for a few years in Toronto, then moved to Vancouver.

When Dad had had enough of trailing everyone around the lake behind the boat, he claimed his turn, then announced teatime and called it quits for the day. Teatime tradition dictated a group swim to Grandpa's island and back. Except for Mom's best friend, Eloise, still quite tentative in the deep water, the multi-generational group set out. One person delegated as the lifeguard rowed alongside the group.

One post-swim afternoon in late August stands out in my memory. I walked out of the water and grabbed my towel off the back of a lawn chair. I heard music. Where could it be coming from? The volume increased. Snippets of familiar lyrics wafted from the direction of our cottage. A distinctive guitar riff rippled down my spine.

"I got the radio working. Your favourite song is on."

Mom called from inside the cottage where she was starting dinner preparations over her new two burner electric stove. I could make out her faint shadow as she pressed the brown plastic Westinghouse radio closer to the screen. Electricity had arrived at Loon Island and with it the raucous tones of rock and roll. Mom cranked up Buddy Holly's new single, "That'll be the Day."

"Makes things easier for our chief cook and bottle washer," Dad said, grabbing Mom in a hug after flipping the switch in the new electrical box. "No more squinting at cards and board games on rainy days." More was over the moon with the new convenience.

Staying up later to read got easier, somewhat. But the light from our bedside lamps illuminated the rafters, visible over the bedroom partitions. "Lights out in there," Dad would call from their bedroom strategically placed between Doug's and the one Donna and I shared. They'd been sleeping inside the cottage for a few years now, mostly to ensure we went to sleep on time. "We'd like some sleep, even if you wouldn't."

Shivering slightly, goosebumps rising in the late afternoon shade, I wrapped my towel a bit tighter and sang along to the prophetic words of Buddy Holly. The legendary pioneer of rock and roll had already left us. Seven months earlier, on February 3, 1959, the Beechcraft Bonanza aircraft Buddy had chartered to get him to his next gig on the Winter Dance Party Tour crashed into a frozen cornfield near Mason, Iowa. Holly and fellow musicians Richie Valens, JP Richardson, known as The Big Bopper, and the pilot Roger Peterson were killed. Holly was twenty-two years old.

Childhood summers seem endless. No more. Buddy was gone. Doug, Donna, Mary and Jamie were drifting away faster than afternoon clouds on a windy day. Roger was rapidly approaching old age. Electricity had arrived. Life at the lake would never be the same.

CHAPTER 36
END OF AN ERA
2008

"*S*ign *there, below the other two signatures.*"

I'm third in line, as usual. The lawyer passes me the document. It's the deed for Loon Island, with the exception of the small section severed for Donna in the early 70s.

That remains hers alone.

In the quiet office conference room Dad, Doug, Donna and I encircle a round table with the lawyer. We're all dressed in casual cottage clothes, T-shirts, and long pants. Except for Dad. Dad's shoulders display his usual ramrod perfect posture. At 92, there's still a dash of pepper in his pepper and salt beard and his wiry gray hair is as bushy as ever. His collared, long-sleeved cream shirt indicates the gravity of the occasion. Shoulders relaxed, he's as ready for the hand-off as he always was on the football field at the University of Western Ontario. The offices of Cunningham, Swan, Carty and Little feature original exposed limestone walls of the familiar Smith Robinson building in downtown Kingston. The new elevators are smoother than the ones when it was S and R. But, definitely not as much fun. No uniformed operator calling out, "Ladies lingerie. Going down."

Mom fought valiantly but lost her long battle with Parkinson's at eighty-five. Dad stayed by her side every day. Now, eight years later, the island isn't the same without her.

"Not a bad deal for one dollar." Dad offers a smile, maintaining a stiff upper lip. I can't imagine what this day must be like for him. The end of an era. "You can pay the taxes now." It's a family joke.

After a decades-long correspondence, sometime in the 60s Dad and the taxmen came to an agreement. We had gone from the original stress of the quit-claim deed not being recognized to the deadline of having to take a second mortgage on the house in Weston to buy the island and build a cottage within two years. Then the discussion – Mom prefers the term discussion to the word argument – about whether the building was a cottage or a screened-in porch. Hassles followed over the high and low water definition of foot frontage around the island, and finally the agreement to pay by the acre. From then on Dad paid the taxes without much comment. I think he missed the debate. Every threat of losing the island drew us closer as a family and further cemented our attachment to the granite under our feet.

Every year since we built our bunkie, Barry and I have offered to contribute to the tax bill. Every year Dad has refused. Until now. There are two properties now. When the number of cars owned by the extended family crowded the side lawn at Elwood and Alice's farmhouse, Dad bought a field from his cousin Keith. The lot across from John Harbor Shales I's farmhouse became the family parking area. Now he's selling us both the island and the mainland parking lot. I've owned property before. This is different. This land is part of me. Its granite stabilizes my bones and strengthens my heart. I am honoured to be a steward of Loon Island, part of the preservation of Draper Lake for generations to come. My hand trembles when I sign below Donna and Doug. We hand the papers back to the lawyer. Dad's shoulders relax as we stand and shake hands all around.

The significance of the occasion begins to sink in. Several days before I watched as Dad stood uncharacteristically off to the edge of the lawn in front of his cottage. A wild game of croquet in session, he appeared oblivious to the activity of a crowd of his descendants. The wistful look in his eyes said it all.

After Mom died, Dad returned to their Snowbird retirement routine of going south every winter. Until he was ninety he drove alone, more than 4,000 kilometres diagonally across the USA from Kingston, Ontario to Palm Springs, California, usually in five days. He stayed at his favourite room at The Motel 6. When they wouldn't offer a weekly rate, he insisted on paying by the day, each day for four months. Every afternoon he hiked in the foothills of the San Bernadino Mountains. He never took out health insurance.

"If I get sick, I'll make a run for the border."

Now, at ninety-two, after a couple of minor vehicular mishaps, he had been forced to surrender his driver's license. Despite repeated offers from various family members to give him a lift from the Kingston apartment he rented after selling the house in Weston, he never came out to the lake again.

2010

A late October wind sends frothy waves against the Front Rock. I clutch one of Dad's plaid shirts close to my chest. We each chose one of Dad's work shirts as a memento when he died a few weeks ago just before turning ninety-four. We're wearing them today. Doug, Donna and I shiver, as much from circumstance as from the wind, in Doug's tin runabout. Our spouses Margo, Art and Barry stand as witness, feet firmly grounded on the granite. Barry lets go of the bow rope and gently pushes the boat out over the drop off.

We're adrift with Dad in a sea of sorrow. For once, I go first, tilting the urn full of Dad's ashes, silently saying my private goodbye, as some of the urn's contents spread over the surface. I thank him for his love, and guidance, an abundance of summers past, and the ones yet to come. Donna goes next. Somehow it seems fitting for Doug to go last. He takes a long time. I imagine he's giving thanks but making promises for the future. For the remainder of our lifetimes we are the stewards of the lake. Other family members will follow. That's the way Mom and Dad would want it.

CHAPTER 37
DEAR DOUG

May 2019

When a parcel arrived from you in late December 2017, I was surprised. We hadn't exchanged Christmas gifts for years. Buried beneath the red reindeer wrapping paper was a framed photo. We're in work clothes, leaning together in front of a rustic wood-frame building, tools in hand. Grey hair signals our age. Our smiles show how much fun we're having. I'm seventy-two and you're seventy-seven. A fan of HGTV, I posted the photo on my Facebook page, using it to begin a series I called, "Senior siblings cottage reno." Season 1 documents the beginning of our renovations of the Loon Island cottage, where we spent idyllic summers. There were five of us: Mom and Dad, you and me and our sister, Donna, the middle child, plus our collie Roger, named for my favourite cowboy, Roy Rogers.

That fall, you single-handedly demolished the back two bedrooms, then hauled loads of wood, glass and nails into your small boat for trips to the mainland. Onshore you wheelbarrowed heaping bundles up the path, filled your truck and drove to the dump, time after time.

You prefer to work alone, but when it was time to reinforce the remaining structure, you called on me. Every day that September, we hammered, scraped flaking paint, sanded and primed the new cove siding that you cut and I installed to replace what had been left to rot since the deaths of Mom in 2000, Dad in 2010, then Donna in 2015. When I showed up at 7:30 a.m., you had already put in an hour of work. You chided me good-naturedly for sleeping in. Each new layer of paint revealed another era of family history. "Remember that tan colour," you said. "That was the last time Dad painted the cottage. He was at least ninety that summer." By ninety-three, Dad's health had waned. I thought of how you and Donna visited him every day, arranging caregivers and keeping me up to date until summer, when I arrived from the West Coast to take my shifts.

Scraping layer after layer, we finally reached the original dark green Dad had first painted the cottage. "That was the summer Dad got the red canoe. You always got to be leader. You got to steer in the stern, Donna paddled bow and I had to sit in the middle," I said in my best whiny little sister voice. The only kids on the lake, we relied on each other for entertainment: fighting, fishing and building forts. You teased me but secretly I adored you.

The boards got a second coat of green the summer you and Dad arrived with the Peterborough cedar strip Aqua Flyer speedboat. You were fifteen. You paid half for the boat, motor and waterskis with money earned as a caddy at the Weston Golf and Country Club. I was so proud of you.

During the winter, at school in the Toronto suburbs, we went our separate ways. But once in a while you took me with you on your paper route on our toboggan, dragging it over snowy sidewalks with me cocooned between stacks of *The Toronto Telegram*. When you were short-handed for road hockey, you let me be goalie. When I had my first job as a basket girl at the Weston swimming pool, you were my boss. Head lifeguard, you included me when the gang went for toasted Danish pastries after work at Weston's legendary Central Restaurant.

As the hammering, scraping and priming of Season 1 drew to a close, we cemented our new relationship—carpenter and apprentice. By midway through Season 2, you were bragging to others about your little sister the carpenter and painter.

As two retired teachers, we honoured recess every day. You brewed coffee. I made cranberry oatmeal muffins. We sat outdoors in the red Muskoka chairs. You outlined our next steps. We discussed paint colours, ice blue for the interior, grey for the exterior. Conservative by nature, you at first resisted my suggestion to paint the screen door red to match the chairs. I won in the end.

Season 2 finished with us re-shingling the front pitch of the roof. We'll be back at it in June this year for Season 3. Still have the back pitch of the roof to do.

Mom and Dad built the cottage so we could spend summers on the island. Now facetiously referred to as the "main lodge", it serves as a base camp for family members who gather for afternoon tea and distance swims. As a father, grandfather, uncle and great-grandfather, you've worked tirelessly to preserve the cottage and family traditions. You're the last to leave the lake in the fall and the first to arrive in spring. And I know it will be your motor I hear in mid-May when I pull into the parking lot to wait for my ride to the island.

(This essay appeared in *Maclean's* magazine in May 2019 as part of their *Before You Go* series, which collects unique, heartfelt letters from Canadians taking the time to say "Thanks, I love you" to special people in their lives—because we shouldn't have to wait until it's too late to tell our loved ones how we really feel.)

Doug and Patti in front of the Main Lodge for
Maclean's magazine. —Barry Hodgins

EPILOGUE

plus ça change, plus c'est la même chose. The more things change, the more they stay the same.

October 2021

The thermometer hanging outside our cottage door reads 8 C. Inside it's 12 C. Not fully insulated, our cottage holds some heat overnight. I pull my chair closer to the cast iron wood stove. Cedar and pine logs crackle merrily. I love being up before Barry. Building the morning fire comforts me. Curling newspaper and arranging kindling log-cabin-style on top reminds me of Dad. He's been gone eleven years now. Mom, almost a decade more.

I leave the fire and walk down to the dock for a morning hello to the lake. Daydreaming and stretching, I see the lakefront properties brothers Bill and Clarence Stoness bought years ago. They subdivided and offered a spot to each of their eleven siblings. The land, barely used, except for camping, remained quiet during my childhood. Our life centred around the lake viewed from the Front Rock. Over the years Stoness family members built cottages. Some stayed, some sold. But, Stoness descendants remain as owners of seven of those lots. It seems the Shales aren't the only ones with a long-standing tradition of stubbornness and connection to the land. Those lucky enough to purchase one of the remaining six spots, like Doug's daughter Kerry and her husband Barry Brooker, honour, in large part, the tradition of tranquility. Most travel in canoes, kayaks or rowboats or the occasional small motorboat.

The view hasn't changed much from the Front Rock. The stately white Victorian built by Grandpa's father William Senior still dominates the landscape. From the kitchen window Cousin Mary and her husband Wayne Newport keep an eagle eye on events on the lake. Four of the rental cottages remain empty. Now in their eighties Mary and Wayne have deemed rental too much of a hassle. Their daughter Wendy built a shoreline cottage between The Coulee and The Honeymoon cottages below the maples of the sugar bush hill. Wendy's younger sister Nancy has taken over The Cedars cottage at the beach. The Aerie has reverted to its original purpose as boathouse storage.

John Harbor's house stands tall beside our family parking lot, almost obscured from the lake by large oak, basswood, pine and maples. Vera, who was born in the house, lives there with her husband Ken Shepherd, stalwart stewards of the original farmland. Their son Leslie plans to build a house adjacent. Daughter Angela lives on a nearby farm.

With the exception of three permanent homes along Shales Road, two formerly owned by Shales, and two islands, one owned by the Crown, the remaining lakefront and islands remain firmly in the grip of the Shales family. As I write I hear the sound of hammering travelling across the water from Grandma and Grandpa's island. Workers are installing metal roof that will protect the cottage for future generations. The cottage has belonged to Doug and Margo for more than three decades now. Last week they went home to Oakville for the winter. Doug will be back Thanksgiving weekend to close up the cottage. We will leave a few days later for the drive west back to SilverStar.

Doug's daughter Drue, her husband Gary Pollenz and their friend Scott Smith bought Turkey Island from the Leighfield family. Drue inherited her eye for design from her mother and practical project skills from her dad. With skill, creativity and a lot of paint she has transformed the once dark cottage into a bright, airy vacation dream. Distant relatives of Aunt Laura, the Robinson family, bought Stonehouse Island, once owned by Uncle Jack and Aunt Laura. Cousin David still summers at Dave and Gladys' cottage on Huckleberry Island, joined to Loon Island by marshy lowland. His brother Ken died three years ago.

Donna left her cottage and portion of Loon Island to her second husband Art. Several years ago Doug and his daughters Drue and Kerry and their spouses purchased the lengthy shoreline fronting the old lead mine. Doug's grandchildren dream of building cottages there. Cousin Ian inherited his grandparents Walt and Hazel's mainland property. "Of course, I'll never sell," he says. "This is Shales country."

Doug and I remain official stewards and caretakers of our beloved Loon Island. We take the responsibility seriously, recognizing our position of privilege of being born into the Shales family. We spent three seasons refurbishing our childhood cottage. Now Doug continues most of the upkeep. Barry and I share expenses and assist, when he lets us. Donna's daughters, Patti, Rondi, Sherri and Lori have free use of it during the summer, as do Doug's children, Dean, Drue and Kerry.

We all still gather at the Front Rock on summer afternoons. At one time everyone knew to show up at 3 p.m. Mom poured from the blue willow tea pot. Dad readied the Aqua Flyer for water skiing. We tend to text each other now to arrange inter-island swim times. We bring our own thermoses of tea, go potluck on cookies and gather around the once white waterskiing disk, nailed to a stump and painted gray to create a tea table.

If not for Draper Lake, I doubt I would know my nieces and nephews so well. I probably would not know my grand nieces and nephews at all.

Mom and Dad created countless traditions that have lasted through the generations. Members of a close extended family, we are grounded by a sense of belonging, an attachment to the land, an almost emotional bond to the granite platform of the Canadian Shield that began with the arrival of our ancestors from Wisbech, England. Their strength and determination carried them through challenging farming conditions and severe Ontario winters leaving descendants with a legacy of resilience.

"Both the original John H. Shales I homestead of Lot 17 in Concession 11 and his grandson William's farm next to it on lot 16 have been in the Shales family since before 1873. Given the strong family ties and the devotion the descendants feel to the land, it is not likely these properties will soon pass into the hands of non-relatives."

From The Enduring Spirit, The History of Frontenac Provincial Park 1783-1990, by Christian Barber with Terry Fuchs. Quarry Heritage Books, 1997.

ACKNOWLEDGEMENTS

When my maternal grandfather, the Reverend James Wesley Ross Gordon, died in 1956 he bequeathed $100 dollars to each of his grandchildren. My parents' only stipulation was to buy something lasting to remember Grandpa. I purchased a typewriter and declared myself a writer. My parents, Doug and Anne Shales, encouraged me from day one.

Fifty years later I finally enrolled in the post-graduate journalism certificate program at Vancouver's Langara College. Thanks to my much younger pals Allison Kabernick, Geordie Clarke, Nathaniel Christopher, Wameesh George Hamilton and Adrian Nieoczym who helped me muddle through that challenging year.

Laurie Carter, TJ Wallis, Glenn Mitchell, Suzy van Bakel, Bobbie Jo Reid, Spud Hilton and Marc Atchison accepted my first freelance queries. Thanks for supporting my earliest efforts.

Thanks to friends Sharonheart, Patti, Karen, Jan and the members of the infamous Waverley potluck posse for always being there for me, listening and encouraging.

Heartfelt thanks to my crew of BETA readers: John and Bev Price, Ellen Rothstein, Joan Stancombe, Carolyn Tanner and Barry Hodgins for their prompt, insightful and constructive feedback. I also appreciate the valuable comments provided on readings of parts of the early manuscript from members of my Write On! Kelowna writers' group. Their enthusiasm for the project and ongoing encouragement kept me on track through challenging Covid-19 times.

Kevin Farrell, Manager of Continuous Improvement at the County of Frontenac Office in Glenburnie, Ontario did a wonderful job adapting local maps to highlight the Shales family heritage at Draper Lake.

I am grateful for the incredible expertise and friendship of brilliant editor and writing coach Sylvia Taylor who provided meticulous editing, suggestions and comments to improve the manuscript.

I am fortunate to be part of the warm and caring Draper Lake community. Past and present, residents and cottagers, blood related or not, they remain my home base and extended family. From the five generations of Shales before me, hardworking farm families, campers, teachers, homemakers and business people, I have inherited strength and resilience and a deep connection to the land we all cherish. It is my hope this book will help to pass this love and tradition to following generations.

Visits around the kitchen table in the farmhouse built by my great grandfather, William Edward Shales, with my cousin Mary Shales Newport and her husband Wayne Newport made me feel as welcome as ever. Thanks to Mary for sharing her stories and photos. Vera and Ken Shepherd invited me to the original John Harbor Shales farmhouse where I spent a wonderful afternoon perusing documents dating back to 1831.

Perhaps the most meaningful and fun part of this project has been sharing memories with my brother Doug through frequent phone and email conversations between Oakville, Ontario and SilverStar Mountain Resort in British Columbia.

And, of course, I am thankful for Barry who built us our own wonderful cottage on Loon Island. Thanks for being my paddling and rowing partner on Draper Lake or as far north as the Yukon River. Your example and love encourage me to keep fit and follow my dreams.

ABOUT THE AUTHOR

Patti Shales Lefkos is former teacher, principal and advocate for inner city children and best-selling author of **Nepal One Day at a Time,** *One Woman's Quest to Teach, Trek and Build a School in the Remote Himalaya.* She is a full-time journalist, author and adventure traveller. Her articles have appeared in *The Globe and Mail, The San Francisco Chronicle, Maclean's, Travelife.ca, Canadian Living, Okanagan Life* and *Okanagan Woman* magazines. She was recently awarded Best Travel Article of the Year in *Postscript Magazine.* When not travelling or writing, Patti loves to ski and snowshoe at her winter home at SilverStar Mountain Resort in British Columbia. In summer she reunites with her extended inter-generational family at her Ontario cottage where she rows, paddles and swims, renewing resilience at her granite island homeland. Profits from the sale of Patti's books support education in rural Nepal.

Visit her at **www.pattishaleslefkos.com.**

INTRIGUED? WOULD YOU LIKE TO VISIT DRAPER LAKE? HERE'S HOW.

Jamie Brick, a descendant of the Stoness family, and his charming wife Annette, offer two highly rated Air B and B shoreline cottages for rent. Have a look. Find them at Draper Lake cottage.

For day-trippers, Jamie and Annette annually host the magical, hugely popular three-day Fantasy in the Forest Art Show the third weekend in July featuring up to seventy-five spectacular artists in the woods near Draper Lake. A second, two-day event happens on Labour Day weekend.

Look for Fantasy in the Forest Art Show updates on Facebook.